Moment of Infinity

ANTHOLOGY OF DAILY DEVOTIONS 1

Andrea Putting

MELBOURNE - AUSTRALIA

First published in 2022 by **Putting Words**

© Andrea Putting, 2022

The moral rights of the author have been asserted.

All rights reserved. Except as permitted under the Australian Copyright Act 1968 (for example, fair dealing for the purposes of study, research, criticism or review). No part of this publication may be reproduced, distributed or transmitted in any form or by any means, including photocopying, recording, or other electronic or mechanical methods, without the prior written permission of the author. All requests should be made through the publisher at the address below.

Putting Words
PO Box 5062
Wonga Park, Victoria, Australia. 3115
www.puttingwords.com
books@puttingwords.com

A catalogue record for this book is available from the National Library of Australia.

ISBN: 978-0-6454591-4-2 (Hardback)
ISBN: 978-0-6454591-5-9 (Paperback
ISBN: 978-0-6454591-3-5 (ebook)

Produced by **Putting Words**

Dedicated to the I in you

Acknowledgements

I acknowledge and pay respect to the Wurundjeri Woi-wurrung people of the Kulin Nation, who are the Traditional Owners of the land where I live, work and find my inspiration. I pay my respects to Elders past, present and emerging of the Aboriginal and Torrens Strait Islanders. I acknowledge their deep connection to this land, water and the spirit of this place.

I acknowledge and pay respects to the Elders past, present and emerging from all walks of life who have taught me and influenced my spiritual journey.

Open yourself up to experience the love, joy and peace that only the breath of the Spirit flowing through you can bring.

4 • ANDREA PUTTING

Preface

The pandemic had hit, and I found myself locked away in my home. People were isolated from friends, family, and life worldwide. Everything as we knew it was whisked away from us in what seemed to be an instant.

It felt like all of the things in life that made my life feel worthwhile were gone. I spent my life serving my communities. Part of that was offering ministry to my church community. Now there was no going to church. How could I serve? How could I share the gifts that were mine to share?

It was early in the morning on Sunday, the 20th of May 2020, when I sat at my computer to write the first of my Sunday Morning Musings. Since then, just about every Sunday morning, I spend time in contemplation and allow whatever to flow to be written. This is what I share on my Facebook page on Sunday mornings.

It was a way to share and continue the ministry that fills my life. I never know what will come. Sometimes it feels repetitive to me. Sometimes I look at what I have written and think it may not make sense. However, these are the times when someone has commented that this is just what they need for the circumstances they find themselves in.

I have learned to trust the flow.

This book is a collection of my writings from 2020. It includes my Sunday Morning Musings and many other pieces that come as I start my day in front of my computer and allow the words to flow.

They are not in any particular order. I invite you to pick up the book and randomly read just one piece. Allow whatever message that comes to you to come. Some may make no sense. Others will hit the spot. Whichever it is, take a moment to tune in to your soul and listen for what it says to you.

I hope you will enjoy and benefit from this selection of reflections, stories and psalms.

Andrea's Path

I did not choose this path. This path chose me. I can try to run from it, but it always beckons me home. "This way, this way, this is your way. This is the only way for you to go."

Sometimes I feel like wandering off in a different direction. Can't I just be like everyone else for a while? Can't I just give in a little? But no, that is not to be. As soon as I step off the path, I feel it calling me back. Its pull is so strong.

It is not an easy path. Many obstacles come up. It feels like there are many tests and trials to overcome. No matter how hard it gets, I keep on going. I trudge through the mud. I wade through the deep waters. I climb the highest mountains. It is sometimes freezing cold and other times boiling hot. It seems like it is easy at other times, and I skip along the path. Then I break into a run, just for the fun of it.

On my path, I am often alone. It is too hard and too long a journey for many. They come for a moment, then take a different route. This is not their path. It is mine.

I am grateful, friend, for your company, even if it is just for a while. You will know, understand, and receive what you need somewhere deep within. You may not understand some of the crazy things I do or say, but that doesn't matter.

When you start to see the Truth of this path, you may not start on the journey. You may choose to turn away. For me, the calling is too strong. The rewards are great, beyond, Anything of my imagination. I will continue on my path all my days. For me, there is no other way.

Be Still

Be still, be present. I am always with you. Let my words
flow through you. I am with you in all that is.
I am here with you.

Be this.

Moment of Infinity

I soften to the moment, surrender to the now. This moment, there is no other. I let it envelop me like a warm blanket, slowly melting into the warmth of my soul. The Spirit fills me with its presence, taking me into a place of allness. The physical form dissipates as I melt into the now. There is only this. It overwhelms the mind and takes it apart. The allness, the oneness is all there is.

Like a molten state, it flows over valleys and mountain tops, taking them all with me and melting them into my beingness. All that I have seen, all that is before me suddenly, is in this molten state of being.

I rest in this place of pure bliss. I see forever. I see infinity. I am this, in this moment. This moment is me. Forever, past and future are me. This pinpoint where I stand is me. The faraway galaxies are me. Right here in this moment, they pour into the oneness that I am.

I surrender to this moment. This moment of Infinity. There is no other—just this.

I Hear You Call Me.

I hear you call me. I am here. I listen for your voice, trying to hear your words. Sometimes I miss them. My thoughts take me off on another journey. Then I have once again forgotten. I have become busy and haven't stopped to listen. I haven't been where I need to be.

My mind likes to take over. My thoughts want to lead the way. "Hurry up, make some plans, act now".

In the silent moment, that split second when my mind stops, the space between breathing in and breathing out, I hear you call me. I capture that moment. I long to be in it. I grasp it as if I am grasping for my last breath, holding on to that moment of infinity that suspends me beyond time.

If I listen, I hear you call me. If I listen, I am free of struggle. If I listen, I can love with all of my being.

Stop and listen, for this is what takes me beyond all that my mind thinks it can be. If only I listen.

Only if I listen can I be all you have for me to be.

Perfectly

Here. Here I am. I may not be perfect in your eyes. Others may see me as broken, uncertain, and maybe even confused.

But here I am. I am perfect. I don't have to be what others think I should be. I don't have to do things the way others do them, for I am me. I am the perfect me. No one else can do me the way I do me. The way I do me is so perfect.

I live in imperfection perfectly. It is whom I am meant to be. This is the way I am designed to show up in the world. When I stop trying to be perfect, I feel how perfect I am. The perfectionist in me, always trying, always striving, stops. I can just be me, perfectly.

No Words

I need no words. I need no thoughts. Just be still. Be in the quiet and listen.

I am present.

My Child

My child, my precious child, don't grieve. Do not rest in the fear and doubts of this. Be in the stillness of it, I will heal your pain, and you shall shine beyond what anyone can see. Just rest in my arms for now, forevermore. I am yours; you are mine. Be still.

One

There is only one consciousness.

It is me. It is you. It is all. There is no separation. There is only this one. The one and only being, the omnipresent. This is who I am. This is who you are. We are.

We think the world is so far apart. We believe we are separated by time and space. We aren't. We can never be separated. No matter how much they try, there can never be separation, for there is only one infinite being. I am this, and so are you. We are one, eternally. The one Infinite child of God.

Let Your Love Shine

Let your love shine through me, God. Let every breath I take be of service to you. Guide me on the path you would have me take and help me let go of those things that pull me away from you.

Be my love, be my lover whom I pour my heart into. I give you all that I am. I give you my all. How can I not? This is what you have given me. You have given me the greatest of everything. It is all laid out for me on a banqueting table. It is there for me to share with the world. It is from my love. It is for my love. It is everything. I am here.

Walk In the Light

Be still. I will guide the path. I am opening the doors for you; all you need to do is follow. I am the way. You are mine. It is all there before you. Just walk in the light.

Let Your Light Shine

Let your light shine. It is time. I have carried you this far. Now it is time for you to walk with me. You know that I will always be with you. I will always give you the words to write and say if you just keep listening.

Take the time, always. Connect with me constantly, and your words will be my Words. Your actions will be my Actions. Your Will be my will. I am here, and you are ready.

Let's start this journey together.

Be confident of my love. You can always lean on me. When you get tired, I will carry you. When you think you have lost your way, I will guide you. Stay on this path with me, and together we will discover new horizons.

Let your light shine, for it is beautiful, and many will follow.

Middle of the Night

In the middle of the night, I stood gazing out the hotel window. The night was still, and the roads were quiet. The city lights glistened as my weary eyes worked on focusing on the details.

As I accept the darkness, there is peacefulness. I find in it a sense of stillness. There is nothing to do, nowhere to go. Just to be in the serenity of being. To be in the quiet.

Here I seek deeper. Seek deeper into my being. Who am I right in this moment? None of the labels that the daytime requires is important here. It is just me. There is no other. No one to question me. No one to take my time. No one to serve. There is no one—just the presence.

The presence summons me into the deep. Deeper and deeper. Here the truth becomes alive. There is no one else, no other. This oneness overtakes my essence—the feeling of oneness with all. Be still and feel into it. Let go of all and just be present. Be still in the now.

Where I am going doesn't matter right here. Where I have been has gone. In this most powerful of moments, I am. Right here, where the presence lifts me and holds me. Right here, I learn that this presence is always with me, always holding me. There is never a moment that is not right here within me. It is me that doesn't recognise it. It is me that hides busily in the world mind. When the world mind is silent, in the depth of the night, I can feel what is lost in the daylight.

How do I awaken to a new day? A new day of being. A day where I can feel this presence that holds and sustains me at every moment. This presence that is truly the essence of my being. I don't want to let go of this moment. I want this to be my everything.

I am beckoned to explore deeper. Can I let go? Can I move into the truth of the night? Can I allow this presence to take over and lead me into the true light of day?

As morning breaks and daytime activities start, it is easy to be once again drawn back into the busyness of the day. So easy to forget this presence that holds me. I forget the message of the depth of the night that through every moment, I am supported and sustained. I am love.

If I just let go and remember, I will be guided into the most glorious of all days.

Peace

Peace. It reigns over my heart. As I look to you for clarity, I find peace. A new peace, a different peace than the world knows. A peace that flows through all things, through my very being. A peace that I cannot comprehend with my mind.

I feel it in my soul. It is here that the Spirit speaks to me. Speaks in true depth. It calls me by my name. It knows me beyond the me that I can ever know. It is me, but not the me that the world knows, the me that is the Spirit, that lives in the Divine.

It comes to me from a place beyond, yet that place is here, right here in the midst of me, from within. I cannot run from it. I cannot hide. It knows my every move and thought and still sits with me, waiting for me to recognise it. To recognise me. The real me. The me that is Spirit. The me that is one with all and flows in the Spirit of all.

Here I find sanctity from all. This peace is here. All I have to do is let go and be.

God's Day

This day. This day is God's Day. It is the day I surrender all. But wait. Didn't I do that yesterday and the day before? Haven't I surrendered all before?

Yes, but the journey continues. Each day, the world mind infiltrates my being, dragging me into humanness. Each day, it is a constant battle to stay in the presence, to stay in the Truth of who I really am in so many ways—the child of God.

Do you remember that? Did you not forget that in every moment? When you spoke to your partner? To your child? To your work colleague? Or the stranger on the street? Did you remember that you are the child of God? Did you recognise that they are the child of God?

Did you remember when you brushed past someone in the shop or cursed that person cutting in front of you? Did you remember when you held yourself up as being somehow more important than someone else? Do you remember?

For these and many, many more reasons, in each and every moment, it is time to surrender to the Christ within. Surrender to the peacefulness and serenity that you can only find at this moment through the presence of God. Allow yourself to be guided and transformed through everything you do. Do not battle. Just let go and allow it to take you where you can be at your best, to where you are meant to be. Surrender to the Christ within, and you will shine your light for the world to see.

Guide Me

Here I am today. Ready to be guided on this path of truth. Show me the way. Show me the path I need to take. Show me what I need to do today, right now. I don't need to know the end destination. I just need the now. I need the reality of the spirit. God, my one true love, open up for me today my truth, the Truth. Don't let me stand still in complacency. Help me to see what I need to see, the truth in all things. I am here, and I am ready. I am open to being your instrument, to do your Will. What is it you want me to do today? Open my heart, my all.

Autumn Leaves

I catch a glimpse of the light that flickers through the autumn leaves. It comes and goes. Sometimes I see a big patch of sunlight. Sometimes it is just a tiny flicker. As more leaves fall, the more I see, the more light is revealed. Somedays, catching that light feels like a battle. I have to chase the light to find just that glimpse. On other days I can stand and bask in the sunlight for hours, feeling its warmth penetrating my being.

As I watch the light flicker, I see the truth of how my life is. Somedays, the light is clear, and I live fully in the Presence. On other days there is just a pin light coming through. These days, I struggle. I struggle to live in the fullness of who I really am. I struggle to connect with my soul's truth, the essence of my being. I struggle to be the light that others need me to be. I struggle to be the reflection of your love.

So, I look for the light. I seek to stand in it, to be it. To take the time just to bask in its warmth. For here is my truth. My very soul longs to be only the light that shines brightly. It longs to share this, the warmth that fills my being. To share the love.

The light beckons me forward, "*Be in the light. Be the light*", it says. "*Others need to find their way. Others need you to surround them with the light, feel the warmth, and feel the love radiating from you. Be this.*"

Never stop believing that you have so much to bring into the world. When you see through the flicker of light, you can glimpse who you are designed to be. You are the light.

Shine.

Lead Me by Still Waters

Lead me by still waters. Take my hand, and I will come with you wherever you lead. I trust in your presence and know you will bring me safely home. You bring me the stillness where we can just be. Here we can rest and connect. The stillness of the waters allows all else to dissipate in my world. There is just this moment. This moment of peacefulness

I shall not want. There is nothing that I can need or want, for you are my everything. My day, my night. My bread, my wine. Everything is here right here in this moment. There is no lack, only light and love. It fills me beyond my beingness. There can be nothing more, nothing less.

Waiting

Where do you want me to go? Who do you want me to be? I can't help but ask every day. I sit in the stillness and wait. I am waiting for the answer. What am I to do today? How can I serve? What is your will for me? I wait.

Sometimes I hurriedly jump up with things I feel I just "have to do." Often, they aren't that important. It is better to wait. I sit in the stillness and feel your love, enjoy the peacefulness of Spirit and allow it to flow through me. I like this waiting. At least, my Spirit does.

My mind is in a hurry. What is it I am to do? Come on, tell me. I need to get up and do something. Anything. I don't want to make a mistake. I don't want to waste time. I don't ………. Wait! Be still. Don't rush away.

In the stillness, there is purpose. It speaks to me with unsaid words. It shows me things unseen. It tells me there is a direction when I see none. I just have to wait and trust. It is there. I am guided. I am on purpose. I am following the path set before me. I am the path.

Stepping Forward

Being in the stillness is stepping forward. All that I am is that moment. That moment of stillness. It calls to me; it whispers loudly in the silence. Stillness is not stopping; it is being still in the silence of the busyness of the mind.

The place I call the City of the Mind is so hectic. It doesn't want to stop. It keeps me running forward. Well, what I think is running forward. In reality, it is just a treadmill that keeps on going around and around. What is stepping forward to the mind is being stuck in one place to the soul. The mind only sees this tiny picture, as if we are in this prison cell that inhibits the greater truth of the soul. It will not let us see who we really are. That is the power of the City of the Mind. It keeps us trapped in this illusion.

The Stillness – the Skill of Silence, opens us up to see what is beyond the city. When we sit in stillness, we can see all that is. Every possibility is opened up to us. There is no more limitation. We are not confined to our prison cells. There is more, so much more. In the stillness, when you start to glimpse infinity, the fullness of the Spirit, the soul of who you really are, you can begin to step forward. Forward in a way that you have never seen before. Forward into the Divine Truth of all that you are.

Doors

I stand before the doorways. There are many. There are many options: which door should I open and which one should walk through. I could run through them without thought, just open a door and go through it.

But I wait. I wait to see which doors will be opened for me. Which door do YOU want me to go through? It is not for me to choose, but for me to be ready to respond and awake when the door is opened. To see through the world and the competing options. They are noisy and distracting. The door You open will be gentle and quiet. I must look, tune out the world and be aware.

Where is the crack of light coming from? I see it in the corner of my sight. As I walk towards it, the world keeps calling, "over here, over here, this door, come through this door." But I keep my focus and walk ever closer.

The light is becoming brighter, and I start to see where it is coming from. The door is opened a little more, inch by inch, with each step. I begin to hear it calling me continuously. *"This is the way; this is your path. Just follow the light, and I will guide you."* Yes, this is the way I want to go. I want to go beyond and be in the light. I want to be in the presence and feel the Divine guidance.

As I reach the door, it is flung wide, and all that I am to be, all that I am called to be, is just that step away. All I need to do is walk through the door.

God, I am yours. Send me where you will. Help me to see those open doors.

Magnificent

As I sit here and reflect for just a moment, I see the magnificence before me. I can be only this, and this is magnificent. There can only be this magnificence that fills my being. It is all-encompassing. It is who I am, all that I am. It is me.

There is no other way for me to be. I embrace the fullness of my being. The fullness of who I am meant to be. All that is wrapped up in this moment. All of it is here right now. It is revealed to me in increments. Bit by bit, I can see it. It is magnificent.

I can only be this. I can only be magnificent.

Grace Accepts Me

Here I am. I am not so innocent. There are so many times I have fallen. So many times, I have made the wrong decision, gone the wrong way and certainly said the wrong thing. My actions have sometimes hurt others deeply. I haven't always thought highly of myself. I have sat in guilt and even pity. I have destroyed myself many times.

Through Grace, I have found my way and seek to be guided. Grace has enveloped me so that I can be free of all this. It opened my eyes when I couldn't see. It has healed the wounds that I now see were often self-afflicted. It has helped me to find in myself something beyond human measure. Something that guides my way and fills my being.

Grace accepts me, always. It doesn't ask what I have done. It doesn't keep a scorecard. It goes beyond my comprehension to where it can see only the good in me. As I feel this grace, I seek only to see the good in others. I try to look beyond the human façade to see only the beauty of the Spirit that lays within.

Grace says to me that I need to look no further for the peace that I had sought within me, for it is always there. It is mine for the asking. All I need to do is to live in this Grace and allow it to flow through me.

What else could I need? I need for nothing as long as I have Grace.

Start with God

As you start your day, what is most important?

Is there anything else that you could possibly need to do? Or to be? The first thing that needs to be what is the priority in your day. What is the most important thing in your life? What would stop the day from being everything you need it to be?

There could only be one thing.

Start with God.

The first thing of all, be in the presence. Listen to the guidance. Be this. Be in this place. Let God take over the day. Let God in to be the one focus of your everything. There can be nothing else. No-one else. Just let everything go. Place it in God's hands where you know that all things are cared for. Let it go. Let it be.

Let it be God's Day. Each and every day. Then you know that everything is in its place.

Reflections

As I glance in the mirror, what do I see? Is that who I am? What does the world see? This is all. Who I am is not this image seen by the human eye. Yet that is the me that people think I am. From this image, they make conclusions. They decide who I might be. They think they know me. It is easy for them to assume how my life is, what I might do, and how I think. They might think I have a certain amount of money and do certain things. But this is not who I am.

Who I am is hidden from the view of the human eye. The me that I am isn't dependent on this outer view. It is only when one is prepared to go deeper, stop and listen, explore, and be present with me that they start to feel who I might be.

Who I am is just like you. With dreams and hopes, with fears and uncertainties.

Who I am desires to be loved, held, and a part of community.

Who I am wants to serve and feel that she has made a difference in the world.

You see, I am just like you. No matter what you see or think I might be, I am just like you. No matter where or how I live, I am just like you.

I Am One

I sing of your love. I sing of your presence. I sing of all that is.

Fill my heart with your presence. Fill my heart with your being. Fill my heart with all that is.

I am yours. I surrender unto you. Hold me in this moment, this moment of infinity. Hold me here. There is nowhere else to go. Nowhere else to be. There is just here in this moment. Here in this moment of un-time. Here in this moment of un-space. Here in this moment of un-ness, I find the
Allness. When I am nothing, I am all.

I release the need to be something and allow the greatest desire of nothing to overtake me. This is the time to be me. This is the time to let it go and live in the Trueness of my being. Just let it go into nothing to find the All.

I am One.

Through the Fog

Morning, the start of the day. I catch a glimpse of the sunlight through the fog. I stand in it and bask in its warmth. The dew sits softly on the grass, and I walk gently on the earth.

Yet, as I feel the peacefulness of the morning, I live not in it. It reminds me of the beautiful presence of the Spirit. It is the Spirit that warms my soul. It is the Spirit that embraces and encapsulates all that I am.

The world that the mind creates can be beautiful. It can be inspiring and uplifting. However, this world can also be painful and absolutely ghastly. There is a constant fight for the good. The good easily turns to bad. How can this be of God?

God speaks to me in the midst of the silence. Lift above this world. It is not mine. My kingdom can only fill you with this sense of wholeness, oneness, love and everlasting peace. A peace you can never truly grasp hold of while you are living in the world. Let the world go. Trust me. Trust the I within to hold you as you cross this narrow bridge.

There is much you want to hold on to. There is much you are fixed to, but it just holds you there in one place. It does not fill you. It doesn't sustain you. It only makes you hungry for more. Let it go now, and you will never be hungry. You will never thirst. *What I have for you will fill your soul with so much love and peace that all that is will be drawn to you.*

Let it go now. Trust the process. Be in the one presence. Be in the one mind, the Spiritual mind that fills your soul beyond all that you could ever believe to be so.

It is yours. It is my gift to you. Won't you accept it now with open arms?

Rest In My Arms

Rest in my arms. Let go of the day. Let go of all your troubles. I will hold them. I will take care of all that weighs you down. There is nothing for you to worry about. There is nothing for you to do. There is nothing for you to struggle with.

Just rest in the beingness of your soul. Here you will find oneness and peace. It is all you need. I have provided for you everything that is required. There is nothing more to do—just rest. Rest here, my child. I am here.

Listen Beyond Hearing

When I stop and listen, really listen. What do I hear?

I have to listen beyond hearing. I have to listen beyond words. I listen beyond silence. In the depths of the silence, there is so much to hear.

I hear the echoes of all time. It stands still, reaching into me and sharing its secrets. It reaches my very soul.

I listen to my soul. What does it need me to hear? What does it need me to know? It speaks to me in the depths of silence. It speaks to me in moments of clarity.

It calls out to me. Sometimes I don't hear it. It is a quiet roar that wells up within. I must listen. I must listen to what it has to say. I must be in this presence, in this moment.

Listen, it cries out to me. It speaks to me constantly. I just have to listen. I just have to hear this message from beyond time, beyond space. It is there for me to hear.

It is there. It is here.

Just listen.

I Can't Not Do It

What does your heart say? How do you really feel? Do you know? Do you know what it is? Have you listened? Really listened?

It is easy just to make decisions and take direction from your mind. It tells you it knows what to do. "I'm in control here. I'm the boss!" All that logical thinking, sorting through the options of why and why not—seeing the way forward and making the choices from what makes the most sense. Busy, busy, busy. "I've got this."

While the heart is calling out, silently screaming out to be heard. "Do you really want this? Is this really what will make you happy? Slowly, quietly, we gloss over that little voice. We hear it less and less until we get to the point where we don't even take any notice.

Listening to the heart and connecting with what is speaking to you from beyond the mind can give a clear understanding of who you are and what will fulfil you. Finding that more profound sense of purpose can't just be thought out. It takes time. It takes the greatest guidance that from within. It is not to be taken lightly. It is not something to jump from one thing to another. It is something that needs to brew up from the inside and come screaming out of you. "This is what I must do. This is what **I can't not do**. This is my direction."

Pondering, take time, feel it. Set aside all you know for now, knowing you can come back to it. When you have taken the time to see more clearly, all those other things will fall into place. You will know which of them to pick up and which to let go of. It will make so much sense. It will be as if someone suddenly turned on the light.

Go within. Listen.

Rest in the Spirit

I rest in the Spirit. All of this world tries to tear me down. It tries to keep me busy doing, achieving, and striving. It removes me from the Truth of who I am. I must rest in the Spirit. Be in the presence. Find the Truth in being.

All I need to do is rest in the Spirit. Allow the Spirit to do the work. Allow the Truth to lead the way. This is the Truth.

It carries me through every moment — if I let it.
It holds me up — if I let it.
It feeds me and provides everything I need — if I let it.

I just have to rest here.

River Flow

As I watch the river flow, I sense a serenity. It seems so effortless, just flowing. There is nothing that stops the flow. Where there is a rock or tree falling in the river, the water flows around it, sometimes over it. It just keeps on going on its endless journey. I watch some debris caught up in the flow. It floats on top of the water, moving without effort or struggle. It is taken to where it will go. It will end up somewhere down the river to be in its right place.

I feel its movement, grabbing hold of me and beckoning me to let go. *"Go with the flow. Do not fight it. Go with the flow of life, for it will take you on the journey to where your life needs to be. Don't try to swim against the tide. There you have to struggle and will have to fight for every breath. Go with the flow of the infinite."*

Sometimes we think we have to go against the flow. We feel like we have to fight against oppression, we have to fight for survival, whatever it is in our life that makes us feel a fight is necessary. This is the flow of human existence. However, this is not the flow of life. The flow that deserves a surrender. The River of the Spirit that leads you safely home.

Allow the water to rush over you. Let the current take you to where it is that will be your safe haven. Allow it to be. Surrender to the flow.

Light Creeps Through

Where will this journey take me today? There are so many things I need to do, but I know what it is that you want me to do is far more important. So. I will wait for you to guide me. Here I am. I ponder your Grace. I ponder what it means. This human existence does not weigh anywhere near the importance of your Will, of your Kingdom.

Deep in the corners, I see the light start to creep through. It reminds me that your Kingdom is here. Your Will is the only Will. I am this. I am not separate from it. When I listen to the Spirit, I am listening to who I am. This grand Oneness that is none other. It is who I am. I am connected to all. No, I am more than that. I am all. This Oneness is who I am. My family, my friends cannot be separate. There cannot be a separate person on the street. There cannot be a separate good guy and bad guy. We are all One. What I see is all me. It is inside of my mind, that is all.

The Truth, the real me, is the Spiritual me. I live to be in this. The One Soul, the One Spirit. That is who I am. Here I am truly free. This is the me I long to express. None other. Just this.

Trust the Process

Trust the process. I hear it so many times, but do I do it? Do I let go completely and allow myself to be guided, directed to where it is I am to go?

Trust the process. Sometimes it hurts. It rocks me at my deepest foundations, moves me, shakes me up. I feel the unshed tears that have been pushed down further and further.

Trust the process. Yes, I said. I surrender. I am no longer driving the bus. I will go where I am led. I will go and be what it is I am to be.

The Universe wrapped up a gift for me in the most unusual of wrappings. I questioned, "Why in this wrapping?" As I unwrapped the layer further and further, I started to see why.

It is time. Time to own this. Time to clear the field so that I can be who it is that I am meant to be.

Then the moment of facing that deepest darkest fear appears before me. You know, that one that I don't even admit to myself. The one I sweep under the carpet. The one that I just refuse to face.

"Lean in, lean into this. Feel it. Confront it. Call it out. Know that this is what you need to be doing, where you need to be right now."

Yes, it is a gift, but to receive the fullness of this gift, I have to be fully present with it. I have to be ready to do the work to take me to where I need to go.

Some may say, "I don't need this." And run away from the battle ahead. But I can only embrace it. I can only take it fully and learn its lessons for me. It is time to take each moment, each opportunity, and face what has been hidden within. I must allow those tears to be shed. Notice those moments of learning. Letting go, again and again, and again.

The time has come, and I am here. Let go and trust the process.

Find Me

Find me in the depths of your heart when you look for me else where you will not find me. You may climb the highest mountains, and dive into the deepest oceans. You might take a spaceship and point it to the furthest star. You will never find me there.

I am here, right here with you always. Clear the field, stop the mind and reach into the depth of who you are. That is where I am. That is who I am.

You may see my reflection when you look into the hearts of others, for I am there too. I reside in the hearts of all, for we are really just One.

So, let's start. Start right here. Turn away from all else, shut down the world and dive right into the depths of your being. You might not get there at first, but that's OK, for I am always here. I am forever waiting for you. I am ready to speak with you, share with you, and guide you on your journey. I will never leave you. I will always hold you. I am here. You just have to go within.

Pull Up the Anchor

There is nothing before. There is nothing behind me. There is nothing. I live in this vat of nothingness. A vacuum that is human life. It sucks at my very being. It tries hard to completely take over my being.

It cannot.

Everything calls me from this void. It carries me into the Truth, into the Spirit. It takes hold of me in this moment in the fullness. It is all that I am.

It is not until I can see that what is surrounding me is nothing that I can find the everything. I need to let go, completely let go of this world of every endless striving and struggling—the pain and pleasure of this being. Then and only then can I start to glimpse the truth.

I need to let go of this shore and sail beyond the horizon, searching for a new land, a new way. As long as I am anchored to this shore, I cannot find the Truth, the way of being that calls me. So, I pull up the anchor and set sail. Set sail for a new home, a new way of being. In truth, in trust, while the seas ahead of me won't always be calm and there will be many times that I am tempted to turn back, I know that I will safely find my way.

Home

I am coming home.

Did you realise you had even left?

Home is not the place where my belongings are, where I sleep, eat, and live. Home is something greater beyond this life. Home is where my Spirit is, where my soul longs to be.

It may sound like I am talking about death, leaving this life, and returning to the heavenly home. For most, this is the only way they will find this home. This is the only way that they will return home.

However, home is within. Home is always there.

I feel like the prodigal. I have taken leave of my home, left my father and all of his riches. He has given me life, strength and provisions for the journey. I have gone out and attempted to live my life my way. What has become of me? How have I fared? No matter what I do, it is never enough. It is always lacking, never fulfilling. It doesn't matter how successful I become or how much human goodness I have. It always returns to be a struggle, and I need to find something to fulfil and satisfy me.

Only when I am Home and can rest in the Spirit can I be at peace. It is here that I find peace. It is here that I find fulfilment. It is here that life is sustained. Here I find that I am. I am all. There is no lack, no limitation. It IS. What else could I need or want? There is nothing. It is total bliss. It is Grace.

God's Grace.

There is nothing more needed once I am Home.

This Home I can find right here and right now. It is in every moment, in my very being. All I have to do is to let go of the illusion of humanness, and I am Home.

With You Always

I, Spirit, am with you always. Never forget that. You are the conduit, the instrument. Allow that to flow from you, through you. Allow your life to blossom and be fulfilled from within. This journey is timeless. There is no need to rush. Listen to your feelings and what comes through you about all things. Never deny your truth.

We have a long road to travel together. Allow it to be what it is. Listen and be.

Wonder

We all sit and wonder. We wonder about our lives. We wonder about the future. We wonder what someone is doing. What will happen, where will you go, what will you do?

We dream of something else. Something other than this moment. Something better, something grander. Something more.

But what else is there? I am here. There is nothing else. Nothing more. Everything that I have right here in this moment is all I can be, all that I can take.

I live in the abundance of this very moment. Right now, I have everything I can need. I have air to breathe. I am warm. I am fed. More importantly, is this moment. As I dive into this moment, what do I find? I find the Life, the Love, the Spirit, the Truth. Dive deeper. If you think you see the Truth, know the Truth, you don't. You must feel the Truth, be the Truth. There is no other. It is just the Truth. Live in it, be it.

It will never let you go. It will never steer you wrong. Be in this moment and allow the Truth to take you where you need to be in this moment.

Juice

What is the juice of life? What is it that will indeed feed and nourish me? There is only one thing – the Spirit.

The manna from heaven. It sustains my life; it is my life. There is nothing else, no one else, that I need to sustain my life.

I don't know what it is I am to do. I don't know how to build this that is set before me. All I can do is lay one brick, piece by piece, as is laid out for me.

I don't know who to connect with. I don't know who has the contacts I need. All I know is that I have to lay each brick one by one.

Trust the process, Trust that I will be guided to the right people at the right time. They will come. They will be here. Each step, one by one. Just put one foot in front of the other day by day.

I am Spirit. There is nothing else I need to do, for all is in its place and waiting for me.

The Edge

I feel like I'm on the edge of the cliff. There is nowhere else for me to go. I can't turn back. I can't return to where I was. Where do I go?

Suddenly every aspect of my life has me on the edge. I cannot give in. I cannot cave in. The voice within me tells me to keep going. Don't turn back. You can't sit still. You can't just stay here on the edge. You have to keep going.

Fear suddenly raises its voice within me. It is not one I usually acknowledge. I have come so far without listening to it. I turn it away. No, I don't need you. I know the truth now. I see through your illusions of trying to pull me back down the mountain. I will not go with you. I must move forward.

The edge is calling.

It calls into the depth of my beingness. I made a choice way back down the bottom of the mountain that now is the time to fly. I have climbed so far. It hasn't always been easy. There have been rocks and ditches to climb over. Sometimes the climb was steep, and I had to rest where I was. Other times it seemed easy, and I could run along the trail. I often felt like turning back or just staying where I was. Just enjoy the view and take it easy.

But the urge was strong. It kept pulling me nearer and nearer. I had to make it to the top. I had to, at long last fly.

Now that is where I find myself. The obstacles have been overcome for me to get here. I see others calling me, "No, don't jump. It isn't safe." But I must only listen to that inner voice that is getting louder and louder, calling me from beyond. *"It is time now. You are ready to fly. I have got you. I won't let you fall."*

As I step out to the edge, I know I will leave everything behind. I am no longer a fledgling. I am ready to fly.

Let's do this. One......Two........Three.

Beyond the Horizon

Beyond the horizon is where my eyes rest, for all I see before me is not of me. What is not of me is not. It is just images of my mind, the illusion of the world mind. And so, I rest my eyes beyond the horizon to where the truth lies.

What is there is my home, my truth, my being. I am not of this world but the Kingdom. I am of the wholeness, the Light, the Oneness. This is who I am. I am.

Come With Me

We started on this journey so long ago. Don't turn back now. I have so much to show you. There is so much we have to do together.

Come with me. Don't stop here. You may think you are tired and need a rest, but I will give you my strength and energy; just ask, and it is yours. There will be no weariness while we walk this journey together, for I will carry you.

Come with me. There are amazing things just around the next corner that will surprise and delight you. Everything is ready for you, just come with me. I will take you to places you have never thought of. I will take you to places beyond anything you have ever seen or dreamt of.

Come with me. It is your time to be with me. I will not let you fall. I will hold your hand when things seem insurmountable. Remember, I am with you. As long as you remember this, all things are possible. Put your hand in my hand, and together we will climb the highest mountains, cross the deepest chiasms, and pass through the roughest terrains. Nothing can harm you or get in the way, for I am with you, and this is your path. We will walk together. You will never be alone.

Come with me.

Just a Minute

Tenderly, tenderly, you call my name. *"Come sit with me. I long to be with you. There is so much I want to share with you, and I so enjoy our time together."*

"OK, but first, I need to send this email. Then I need to put the washing on. Make a phone call……..." The time slips by as I hurriedly tend to the things of the world.

"Come sit with me."

"Oh yes, just a minute."

"Come sit with me."

The message keeps coming, but I keep rushing from here to there, never quite getting things right. "What was it I was going to do?"

"Come sit with me."

I have a minute. Then I have to....

"Come sit with me."

It is time to surrender. Surrender to the call of *"Come sit with me."* To take time to listen, to feel the presence of God. To remember what it is that is most important. It is not the things of this world but the gentle guidance of the Spirit. Where will it lead me? Where is it that I really need to be?

Is there someone I need to just sit with? How would I know if I didn't just answer the tender call, "*Come sit with me?*"

I surrender. I listen. Where is it you want me to be? How do you want me to respond? I am yours, send me.

"Thank you, come sit with me, and I will share the Kingdom of Heaven with you, right here, for I am your Parent. You are my child. All I want is to surround you with love. Come sit with me and allow me to fill your Spirit, and it will flow to all beyond this time and space."

"Come sit with me."

Disrupted

I thought I would take my morning as usual. Take some time to be still and present. Spend some time journaling before I start my work for the day. Obviously, that is not what you had in mind. A call came from someone wanting to talk. Someone was feeling lonely. Someone who needs to know that someone is listening to them. Someone who has excellent ideas and vision, yet very few take him seriously. Someone needed me this morning, and I was there.

I was in the presence, following my calling, doing something important. What If I had looked at my phone, seen who was calling and thought, "oh no, it is time for me to meditate." How is that of value to anyone? Now at this moment, this is who I am being called to be. The minister, the listener, the presence. This is who I am.

I listen to the words that you are sharing. Is there something I need to hear? While I am listening to you, validating your sense of being and worth, is there also something for me to take away? What is the message you are sharing with me? I ponder.

There is always something. Something more for me to connect with and understand. I am here, and I am listening.

Darkness

The darkness of the cold grey sky came over me. It penetrated my being. I sank slowly into the blackness. It felt heavy. I felt like I couldn't move. Nothing was going to pull me out of this.

How would I see the sunlight again?
How would I feel the warmth radiate through me?
How would I lift above the clouds?

I couldn't see you, but you were there. You are always there. The Spirit of all is always there. Always with me. Holding me, carrying me when it feels as if light has left me.

I know that you are always with me. I just sometimes get lost in day-to-day life. I get lost in a lonely moment. I feel helpless and hopeless. I feel it could completely swallow me up.

As I feel embraced by your love, the warmth starts to return to me. I see a break in the cloud. The light begins to flicker through. Slowly the light returns. The Sunlight begins to emerge. The warmth returns to me.

Your love and light fill me once again. There is nothing I can't do or be. All that is is before me. I feel the warmth take over.

The Rain

As the rain falls, my heart is filled with your love. I sense the newness, the freshness of the morning. With it, I feel you. I know your presence. It is here. In this moment, I can want for nothing. I feel it flowing through me. I am here. It calls out. I am here to be in your fullness. I am here to love and be love. There is nothing else I can be.

This love surrounds my greatest moment. It fills who I am. It overflows like the water flowing off the saturated ground. It flows down the hill to fill the watercourses. It feeds the thirsty and nourishes the earth. This is your love. Your love flows from me to those who are hungry for your Spirit. It flows through me to those who a thirsty for your Love. It fills the dams and empty spaces and nourishes the soul, for all is here. All is love. The earth is revitalised, and the soul is filled.

The Moment Has Come

The moment has come. I can only be right here. I have lived my life for this moment. This moment is my moment. My moment to be everything I am. Everything I could ever possibly be is right here in this moment. I am ready for it.

Right in this moment, there is perfection. It is shining brightly through me. It radiates like the sun. It is pure. It is the light. It is all.

Everything I thought I wanted to be, is right here. Everything I thought I could never be, is right here. Everything I could have possibly dreamt of is right here.

I am here in this moment, and all that is meant to be is me. I surrender into this moment, for here I am. I am made for this moment. It is my moment to be in my glory, in all God's glory. I am this, I am.

This moment has come, yet this moment is the only moment. The moment of all time. I am always in this moment. I am always in this moment of Infinity. In every moment, I am always the perfection of God's child. It is.

I Dwell in the House of the Lord

God's presence fills me. I can only live here. Here is the fullness of life. The fullness of allness. There is nothing else.

God's love surrounds and engulfs me. I am taken into the holiness of places in every moment. When I live only in the house of the Lord, my cup overflows with grace and mercy. I am all that there is. I am the brightness. I am the light. I am eternality itself. God's house has all, is all. There is nothing else I need to be or do. All is in abundance. I just need to be here and fill my life with your presence. This is all that there is.

I dwell in the house of the Lord.

I Seek My Path

I seek my path. I stop in the morning light and look up to feel the sun on my face. "Am I going in the right direction?" I ask. In the moment of peaceful reflection, I feel a sense of "rightness." A feeling of YES. Keep going. The pathway is unfolding before me.

I look towards the horizon. I try to work out where this path is leading, but it quickly becomes fuzzy in the beauty of the hue. The sunlight is so bright I can't make out any details. I take time to take it all in. To feel the truth, the love, the blessings of this path.

I try to anticipate what this journey may look like. Who will I meet? What do I need to take with me? What preparation do I need? Something comes over me. The answers are clear.

You will meet who you need to meet, those who will help you and those you will help.

You don't need to take anything; everything is supplied on this journey. Anything you do take will weigh you down. Let go of it all and travel lightly.

You have done all the preparation you need. All you need to do now is trust that it is all laid out before you and ready. It is time to put one foot in front of the other.

You are not alone on this journey. You are guided. You are supplied. You are all you need to be. It is time to set forth. Let go of all and walk.

Spirit Fill me

Only your Spirit fills me. Your Spirit is all there is. It holds me. It guides me. It is me.

I open up to allow it to take my all. To take me to where I have never seen before. It takes me above and beyond this world. This is all there is.

My heart is filled with your love. This world disappears. There is no other life that can hold me. My beingness is yours.

It is one. Only one. I feel it. I surrender to it. Take me, use me. Let my life be yours. Let your Will be the only will I know.

I Sit with You God

Here I sit with you God. What shall we do today? There are things on my agenda, but before I do any, I want to be with you. I want to spend my time in your presence in every moment.

God, my lover, my one and only. The one and only. I give myself fully into your presence to be at one with you now and always. I give my all. How can I give more? Tell me, God. I am yours completely. I surrender my allness to you, to give you, to please only you. How can I deepen my love?

I see something open up. I feel it deep in my core, soul, and beingness. The only beingness there is. I feel you calling out to me.

I sense that I am doing right but feel I need to do more. More and more. Give more, be heard more, see more. Then I feel the calmness. Those who are to see me will see me. I will reach them. My job is to be, to be the presence. To be the light. To hold them in the allness of God.

Here I am, God. Guide my every move, my every moment. Place me where you want me to be. I know there is only this, and it is all I will live.

Good Morning God

Here I sit again with you. I am ready to honour you and follow your direction. Leave it to me, and I will stuff it all up. My day will be wasted. But I know my day will be guided if I start with you. It will be helpful. I will be helpful. I will touch the lives of others and fulfil your purpose. I will be with you. You will send me where I need to go. You will place me where I need to be. You will have me speaking to those with who I need a conversation. I will make the difference I need to make.

God, guide me in this moment. I am ready to be your servant, to do only your will. Let me be your instrument. I am here. I am yours.

I Will Guide You

Be silent, dear one, and I will guide you. Be here with me, and I will guide you. You are my child. I love you and provide for you all that you need. Let it all go, knowing that in this oneness, you are mine. Feel me in everything. I am always with you.

Fill My Heart with Awe

Fill my heart with awe. Awe of the magnitude of your love. Awe of the beauty of infinity. Awe of your Grace.

I am but nothing without you. In your Spirit, as one with you, I am all. This awe astounds me. It takes hold of me and brings in to the beyond where I can be in the oneness, where I can see into the greatness of being.

The Spirit fills me with this awe. With every breath, in every moment, I am whole within you. I am here, and you fill this. There are no gaps. It is just in the allness of your beingness that I find my true self, my true path. I walk with you.

Ponder

I ponder life. I ponder the known. I ponder the unknown.

I ponder who am I. What is my calling? What is my message?

I ponder it all.

Then I let it go. I let it flow through the moment of infinity. I don't have to think about it. I don't have to know the how or the why. I just let it go. In this moment, I know there is only One. Only One to lead me. Only One to guide me. This One is All, with me. There is no other—just the ponderous of this moment.

Everything that ever was is now in this moment. Everything that will ever be is in this moment. I don't have to look any further. It is here. It is now, right here in this moment.

I will ponder further. I will take time. I will walk outside of time and space and feel into this oneness of all. This is it. This is all. I live here, in this moment of infinity.

v

Day After Day

Day after day, I am here. I sit and reflect. I take a moment to be in the light, to turn on the light and turn it up a little bit brighter. I have been here for a long time, but such a short time. There is so much to do but nothing to do. There is so much to discover, but I know it all. I have seen it all. There is so much to say, but all I need to do is sit in this silence. This silence is me.

Where do I go next? There is nowhere to go. You are already here. You are everywhere.

What do I need? You need nothing. It is all here. Everything you need is right here. Sitting here with you. It is all.

What do I need to learn? Nothing. It is all here.

Never doubt. There is nowhere to go. Nothing you need. Nothing to seek. You are here. Be.

Relax In the Spirit

Relax in the Spirit. Allow it to take you where it wants you to go. Allow the freedom and bliss to take over your life. Allow yourself to just be present in this moment.

Spirit knows what you need to do, and what needs to be done. Let it go and be guided by this everlasting peacefulness filling your being.

Feel it? It is there whenever you let it go. It fills you up. Know this. Trust this. It is always ready, always present. It is who you are. Just rest in this presence as you go through your day and life. Everything is here. Everything is within. Everything is who you are.

Just rest in the Spirit and let the world take care of itself.

Be In the Presence

Be in the presence. Listen intently. I am guiding you always. Stop to be in my presence, and I will be there. I am all, so that is where I am. You cannot escape me any more than you can escape breathing. I am your every breath. I am here.

Timeless

What is this life? It is a reflection of being that has been rippled and tainted by the refracted light. Until the stillness comes and the skies are clear, we cannot see the truth.

In the still waters, I catch a glimpse of who I am. The reflection that is pure and clear. I can see the beauty and the depth of being. I can feel the light penetrate through to my soul.

These moments are pure and precious to behold. I can see beyond this world, time, space, and who I appear to be. Here I feel that I am One with the Truth of my being.

As I sit in the reflection, time stands still. Forever is in this moment. I am all that I need to be. All that I am, all that I can ever be, sits with me. The vision of the future is right now. Timeless. Limitless.

I hold on to this moment. I don't want to let it go. For here is who I am. Here is where I find the peace that passes all understanding. There is nothing to do, nothing to be, nothing to have, nothing to need. It is all here, with me, within me. It is all.

Lean In

I lean in. I lean into the future. All I need to do is listen. Listen to where it is guiding me to be and to go. Listen to the power that projects from there. It is calling me. Calling me to see new horizons. Calling me to see beyond time.

From the future, I can see the roadmap to follow. I can see where the past has taken me. I can see where I am now. I can see the path that is needed to travel into now.

Where is the future guiding me to be right now? When I see it, not from a place of setting goals, but from a place of this is the direction. It shows me new things that may seem impossible. All I can do is embrace this new vision. I know that this is where I am right now. This place of the future that draws me in and sends me forward.

It tells me to trust. I can't see how this will happen. I can't see all the pieces, but the pieces will arrive in time, in perfect time, each falling into place.

All I need to do now is trust that each step will be laid out before me. I just have to take each step and embrace the richness of the journey.

It is my journey, and it starts now.

The Mountain Top Calls Me

I need to reach the top. Continuously I find myself there, reaching higher and higher. To get to the top, I need to traverse some rugged terrain. I have to give up so much and just focus on getting there. Sometimes it seems too hard. There are too many rocks in the way. The path is too steep. I can only take a few steps, and I have to rest.

I seem to do much resting as I make my way higher and higher. Every now and then, I stop. I look out at the view. Am I there yet? It is so beautiful here, will this do? Can I stop here? Is this far enough?

"No, you have further to go. Keep going," the voice inside me says. So, I pick myself up and continue on the journey. "Isn't there something else I should or could be doing?" I ask myself. The voice reminds me, "This is the only thing you should be doing. The only thing you need to do." And so, I climb.

As I reach higher and higher, everything seems to fade, like a distant memory. The world below just disappears. Just like when the cloud covers the mountain tops, and we can't see it clearly, the world below is covered in clouds. The distractions of the world below are removed from view.

I continue my journey. I continue to climb. Will I ever reach the top? Will there be a time I get to sit on the peak and see beyond the horizon? I keep on going.

My mountain is not a physical one. It is a Spiritual one. It beckons me forward each and every day. Some days I don't feel like climbing. Some days I want to give up and go down that easy slope. But the voice inside me keeps me going, keeps me climbing. Some days I know that I am being carried up the mountain. Some days I feel like I am flying.

My journey continues. As long as the mountain calls to me, I will keep climbing. The mountain is there, and the view beyond the horizon grows forever clearer.

Oneness

I dissolve into the Oneness. I see the world with new eyes. Eyes that aren't of this humanness. Eyes of the Spirit. Everything dissolves into this peacefulness. I feel your presence. I feel you. I stand at the edge with you and call you into the presence. Here we stand together. However, this together is light. It is not separate bodies standing next to each other but an infusion of Oneness. We dissolve into each other.

There is no separateness. We are one here. Just one. One in the light of truth. One in the peacefulness of all.

Just Breathe

The world is standing still while it appears to spin wildly out of control. There is no growth, no movement—just stagnation. We think we are moving forward, but we just spin around aimlessly. One step forward is just another step back around in circles. We struggle and strive to make that next goal, to buy the next thing. We conquer that space just to feel that empty space again. What is the next thing to struggle and strive for? Forever trying to feel that emptiness that haunts us.

Taking time to step outside of this endless circle allows us the space to breathe. The space to stop spinning on the spot. The space to see beyond that treadmill of life, constantly moving but never getting anywhere.

Stop and breathe. Stand still. Take a deep breath. Relax into the freedom that this brings. There is no more to do or try to be. Just be. Just be in that moment and feel into it. It will open up something new and wonderful for you to experience. Just be.

There is no great next thing. You are that great thing. You don't need to be anything more than you are because you are everything and beyond what you need to be.

Just breathe into it. Feel it. It is you. It is now. It is all.

Carry Me Today

Carry me today. I feel that I can't make it very far. Can I just sit here on the side of the mountain? Come back and get me later. It feels like too much. Can I just go to sleep here and turn off the world? I feel weary. The load today feels like it has been too great. Can I put it down now?

Let go of your burdens. I will take them from you. You don't need to carry them. You are not alone. I am always with you. Feel my arms around you when you are lonely. Know that I will always provide rest for you. Come, take my hand, and we will walk together. Leave your burdens here. You don't have to bring them with you. I have taken care of them. We will take the slow, easy road today so you can rest. Rest in my arms. Hold on to me. I will never let you go.

I Am I

I am I. I am not me.

Here I am in this moment, but no longer can I claim to be me. I am beyond me. I am I. That is who I am. Layer by layer, piece by piece, I let go of what was, what is the human dream and walk in the reality of the Kingdom.

Here I am. Here I am I. Nothing else can be. I live only as I. I used to live as the world would have it. I was thrown around from one thing to the other, thrown around like a feather in the wind and subjected to the whims of the world. I never knew from one moment to the next what was coming. I was constantly destabilised by the world.

I needed. I wanted. I was constantly looking for something better, striving for success, and continually looking outside of myself—yearning for that greatness.

Now I sit in silence, in the peace of the stillness. There is calmness. The storm is not I. I am the stillness in the eye of the storm, unmoved, unaffected.

As I step out into the world, I go as a beholder. I see the fear, the tumult, the anguish of life. I see the troubled minds, the push and pull of life. Calmly I walk through it. It is not I. It used to be me, but it is not I. I walk outside. I walk beyond the me of the world.

Now I sit in I. Today I am I. I was I yesterday. I am I tomorrow. I have always been I. I will always be I. For eternity there is only I. This is who I am.

Love Divine

You are love divine. I have made you, and you are mine. You are the very part of me. I cannot leave you behind. You have been with me throughout all time. There cannot be anything else. All of the time. We always have been and always will be. We are one.

Go in my name, for it is yours. Love, live, be.

Be the light that lifts others up.
Be the power that heals the brokenness.
Be the love that fills the world.
Be the peace that fills the emptiness.
Be the stillness where all are one.
Be the one. For all are one, feel the oneness. Live in the oneliness.
Be this at all times, for there is no other time. It is you. It is I. It is one.

I Am Yours

My heart is filled with love for you, God. There is only you. There can be no other, as there is no other. Fill my heart with your love. Show me how to serve you, how to walk with you. How do you want me to serve you? I pour out my all to you and completely give myself to you. Show me your way, your will. How shall we spend the day together, dear God? I am yours; use me.

There was this one time when I could not see. I was lost and lonely. I felt like I was lost in the midst of the crowds. But now I see through that and know where I am, you are. You have always held me, always had me. I am never alone, for you are with me.

Only God

There is only the essence of God.

Everywhere I look, everywhere I am, there is only the essence of God.

The trees that speak to me fill my heart – only God.

The birds that sing that fly through the sky – only God.

The friends who reach out and touch me, and hold me – only God.

My family that holds my heart – only God.

This is the true essence of my soul.

The victim and the abuser – only God.

The body that aches, decays, deteriorates and dies - only God.

The sickness and disease – only God.

The virus that scares people around the world – only God.

Those who would control the world – what are they trying to control? Just a dream. They grab it with their hands, and just like a mirage, it dissipates. There is only the essence of God.

What else could there be? There is no good or evil. No sickness or health. Opposites truly are the same – they are the essence of God.

Let It Flow Through Me

God, let your love, let your will flow through me. I am your servant. What does my human mind know? It is just the shell. Only you can fill my substance with my beingness—only your guidance and direction to take me to where I am going. I know only you. Let it flow through me. Let my will be only your will. Let my eyes see only your light. Let me travel only in your direction, for I am. I am your child. Let the Spirit flow through me. Let it be me. Help me to remove all resistance to you. Help me to be your light, your vessel of truth. I am yours, and you are mine. We are one. I live in the oneness of allness. Let it flow through me.

Spirit Flow Through Me

Where will the Spirit lead me today? I ponder. I allow the Spirit to flow through me. Guide me to where I am to be. Lead me to those who need me. Allow your words to be my words.

I release my will into yours. Let Thy Will be done. I can only do that if I let go of my wants and needs. When I focus I what I want, life becomes chaos. When I let go, really let go, then flow begins. There is nothing I can want or need when focusing on your Will.

Your Grace fills me. It leads me beyond my imagination. The things of this world cannot fill this greatest desire. They cannot hold me. They cannot fulfil me. Only your Grace can be the centre of my life, the well where I draw water.

The well is deep.

Soul Dweller

I am Soul. I live in my soul. I work from my soul. It is all I can be. I cling to my Soul. I will not let it go. I cannot return to simple human existence. I cannot live in that place of illusion and walk around blind to reality.

I am Soul. This is who I am. My one goal. My one desire. Walk in this place of the soul, in the Kingdom, in reality.

I am Soul. I am no longer one of the billions but the one—the only. There is only this oneness, this allness.

I am Soul. It fills my everything. It is my all. I can only be present in soul.

I am Soul. There is nothing I can want. There is nothing I can need. There is nothing I desire in this world of illusion. It can never satisfy me. It can never sustain me. Everything in it is just a fleeting moment followed by another need, another desire. In soul, there is only blissfulness that sustains me always. This is the place of Grace. There is nothing else, no need for anything else.

I am Soul. Here I live, here I will stay.

I am Soul.

Light Finds a Way

The light is so bright that I can hardly see. The world is blocked out. There is only light. How can the light shine so brightly in the midst of this craziness of this world?

The world seems like a dark and dreary place. Sometimes there appears that there is no light. No light to be found. Only darkness and despair.

Yet through the clouds comes the light. Through the slightest crack, it cannot be stopped. It shines brighter and brighter and pushes its way through. There can only be this light. Gradually it takes over. All of the darkness slowly fades as the light infuses every corner. Every being is fueled and warmed in this light.

The darkness can never win. The light always finds a way.

Be Present

Be present with me. Be still, and you will know. You will know what to say and what to do. Be still. Be present.

Hold me in your heart, in every moment. Hold this love and presence. Don't let the world interfere. Now, this moment is Divine. Stand here, be in the divinity of every moment. Don't let it go. It is all you need. Be Divine. Be Pure. Be Holy. This is who you are. Do not depart from this. Be this. You are this. There is nothing else but this. It is you.

Be still.

Let your words be my words. They will flow like a river flowing downstream. Hold them. Allow them to be. You are in the oneness. Be this.

What Do You Want?

I hear these words frequently. What do you want? What do I want? I long to be present. I long to be in the presence, to feel the warmth of God's arms. I long to be all. I long to be connected, to feel the connection of all. To be wrapped up in the Oneness that calls to me.

What else could I want? When I have this allness, there is nothing else. There can be nothing else. All that I can possibly need is contained within the allness.

How can the child of God need for anything, want for anything? There is nothing else. Just let go and surrender to the love and light of One.

Here I am. There is nothing. Nothing of this world. I am this. I give my all to my beingness of this one pure light.

I relinquish the other. I relinquish this world. I am not of this world. I am Spirit. I am One with All. I give it my all.

I am yours, the One, the light, the child of God. I stand here waiting for your love to fill me and take me into the fullness of all. I surrender to this fullness of my being.

I am in awe of God's magnificence. It surrounds me in every moment. It lifts me up into the heavens when I walk in the deep ravines. It fills my soul with unlimited joy. It fills me with completeness beyond my humanness's capacity. It is here, through all my adversities, through all my triumphs.

Often it questions me. Why do you allow yourself to walk away, to be distracted? It tells me there is no need to walk through the ravines and go through all the trials. Just walk in the magnificence of God. For here, you will be lifted up and through all the tribulations. You will see the Truth, the Truth of Life. Real Life. The Life of the Spirit. The Life that is All and All that is you. There is no separation. There is no other. Just let go of the illusion of the self and move into the Self, for you are free to be. Just BE. Be All, for I AM.

Do Not Rush Today

Do not rush today. Slow down. Take your time. Spend some time with me. I will take care of everything, and it will be done. But first, let's connect and allow the presence to flow through us.

Hurry up, slow down. It is time to allow the Spirit to take the lead. Allow the Spirit to take over. Just let it flow. Let it be in the fullness of life, in the fullness of time. It is your time to just be.

Do not rush today. We have plenty of time.

Now In This Moment

Now in this moment, I am being called forth. Called outside of time to be, share, give, and bring God's presence.

Right now!

This is all that there can be. I can only be in God's presence, for that is all that there is. Only God, only Oneness. To live in the Kingdom continuously. Only this. Only God. How can it be anything else?

I surrender unto thee. Take my life and make it yours. Show me where you want me to be. Give me the guidance. Don't allow me to be anything else but yours.

I am yours. Let your love flow through me into the world. Let me be an endless stream of your Spirit that fills the core of each one. Let me feel that soul connection that is the Truth, the light.

I am yours, God. Help me to live in this Truth in every moment.

The Narrow Path

Is this the path that beckons me? I see it ahead. It is narrow, and I can't see where it leads.

The path I am on is quiet. It calls to me. Deep in the forest, I go, deeper and deeper. I can't see where it is leading me. I just know that I must go. People ask me, "Where are you going?"

"I'm going this way", I respond.

"Yes, but where are you going? What is the destination?"

"Where ever it leads."

In a world that tells me that I have to set goals and direction and know exactly where I am going, I surrendered. I don't need to know where this path will take me. I just need to know it is my path, and I will follow it.

The path is narrow. Sometimes it is easygoing. Other times it is so hard. But it is mine to travel, and I know that as long as I stay with it, where I am going will be filled with wonder and awe.

"Go deeper", it calls to me, "Go deeper."

Deeper into the unknown. Deeper into what can't be seen. Deeper into what the world can't understand.

As I surrender again and again to the depths of the unknown, the light becomes brighter. The path becomes clearer, and all doubt and fear are suspended. I walk straighter, stronger into the place of Truth. Here all things are known.

The journey is rich and full of beauty. I behold and stay true to this path.

Take My Day

Monday morning has come around again. I have a new day ahead of me, a new week. There are many ways I can spend it. There are many things to do and that I can do. What is it that is most important?

I give my life over and over again. I give it to God. Lead me in this day. What is it that you want me to do today? What is it that you want me to do this week? I give it to you.

Take my day. Take my week. Take my life. Let me be of full service to you. Let my life be a reflection of you. A reflection of your love. A reflection of your Grace. There is nothing else for me to do or to be.

I am yours, God. Guide me.

Stay in Tune

It takes work to keep your instrument in tune. It takes work to get the tune right and perfect it.

Day in day out, you need to rehearse. You need to get the tune right. You need to try different tonalities, and different paces. It is an endless task of working on perfecting your craft. If you stop playing this tune that is your song, gradually, the skill drops away. You stop being able to play that song with perfection. You have to start again.

The tune I sing is the song of my soul. Each day, I must return to it like it is a brand-new tune. Sometimes I feel like I have it perfect. Other days I feel like I am starting from scratch. It is the tune that calls out to me, "play me, again and again." Play this tune. Sing this song. It may not be perfect today, but it will be stronger and clearer tomorrow.

It will be there when the world calls you to sing your song and play your tune. You have practiced and practiced so that it has become a part of every ounce of your being. You no longer have to think about each note, but the melody flows through you as if you are in automatic mode. You have become this song. It sings out of you without any thought. It is you.

Without this daily tuning up, how can I call on it? I know it is there. I don't have to think about it. It just is. It is now everything I do, everything I am.

This is my song, and it will forever flow out of me.

Sitting in the Light

There is a day. There is a time. That time is now.

I am sitting here in the light. I feel your presence surround me, fill me. There is nothing else that I need to be or want to be. I can just sit and be.

It is incredible to think that I would have been stressing and striving not so long ago. I have to do this. I have to do that. But now I know I don't have to do anything.

I know the greatest power, the greatest wisdom, comes from letting go. I just let it all go. All that is of value *IS*. It just is. It all exists in the now. I live here, on purpose, in peace in the now. My life is content.

I give all to now.

My Heart Calls for You

My heart calls for you. I want to fill you with my love. I want to give you the fullness of my abundance. Everything is for you, my child. Everything is yours. There is nothing I hold back from you. There is nothing I cannot give you. I give it all to you freely. All you have to do is open your arms and receive.

Why do you reject my Love? Why do you reject my Grace? Why do you reject this gift of life that I have given you? Instead, you go on blindly, struggling.

You call out my name, yet you do not look or listen. I am always here. Just stop and listen. I am with you. Always.

Stop and be in the fullness of my presence. Receive this gift I freely give you. Receive this gift of Love, Life and Grace. It is yours.

Allness

What can I be?

Is there anything I can't be?

Is there anything that can't be?

I see that all is. So, there is nothing that cannot be. It all is. All is All.

It is interesting to sit and ponder how everything I see appears separate and individual. Yet the truth is somewhat different. The truth is far greater beyond our human comprehension. The truth is that all is one. How can that be? I am me, and you are you. How can we be one? How can I be the one with you? How can I be one with the murderer, the rapist, the child molester? I certainly don't want to claim that as being me.

Yet, the Truth is that all are One. All that I see, all that I know is one. Then, the truth must be bigger and more incredible than I could have imagined.

If all is One and all is God, then are you saying God is the murderer, the rapist, the child molester? No, God is not that. Then how can it be?

Yes, the question of all ages. How can it be?

It takes a lot to even scratch the surface of this. It is so infinitely big that our human minds just can't take it in.

What does that mean to me? What does that mean to who I am? To whom you are? What does that mean to the way I treat the other? The way I treat the Earth?

But, there is no other. They are me. That is a massive concept. I can't grasp the fullness of it. I try. I look beyond the humanness and seek out the soul, the Spirit. Who am I, really?

It is beyond the human mind. The only way to take hold of it is to let go. Completely and totally let go of the need to understand. Let go of the human mind that tries desperately to comprehend what it is incapable of comprehending. Just let go. Let your soul guide you. Let your soul show you the way.

Sit in the silence and let the world pass by. Sit in silence and invite the Spirit in. Sit in silence and find that stillness within. Let All that is take you to the place of allness.

I Spirit Am Here

I Spirit am here. I am always here. I am here in the darkest moments. I am here in the light. Where ever you are, I am here. It is always Spirit in every moment. I am always with you.

You can try to run, but I am here. You can try to be separate, but I am here. You can try to hide, but I am here.

You and I are One. Open your eyes and see. Open your ears and hear. Open your heart and feel. You will find me.

You don't have to seek me out, for I am here. You don't have to go on a search, for I am here. You don't have to spend your life on a long, arduous journey, for I am here.

I am always here. I never leave you.

A Moment Ago

A moment ago, I forgot. I forgot who I am. I forgot that I am. In that moment, the world started to cave in on me. It made me think that everything was too much. I began to think, "I can't do this" I started to think I have to fight to make things happen.

That was a moment ago. Now I remember that is not who I am. I am one with the Spirit. In this moment, I know that all is possible. I don't have to struggle. I don't have to fight to make anything happen. I just have to rest in the Spirit.

Here in this place, I find peace. I find myself. I find all that is. I can let go. Surrender to all that is.

Here in this place, all that I need to be, all that I need to do is revealed.

Here in this place, all is possible. Everything is opened up to the truth that all is. There is nothing outside the realm of possibility, for it is Spirit that does the work.

In this moment, I rest, sit in peace, and allow the Truth to wash over me. All that *is* is.

Spirit will lead the way.

Surrender

I am satisfied to be what you want me to be, go where you want me to go, and do what you want me to do. There is nothing else for me to be, do, or go, for I am yours, and I surrender all of my humanness to walk in the Spirit.

I can surrender, knowing with certainty that you are there. You take care of my every need. I have nothing to ask for, for it is all supplied before asking. I surrender into the bliss of this beingness, knowing that all are cared for. All is. I can rest in your arms and just be.

Surrender into the arms of God. This is the only place to be. This is all I am. Here I am at the peace of allness. The peace that the universe is at one. *Yes, surrender into my arms and feel the safety of my being.* Surrender into safety. Surrender into peace. Surrender into the almighty, the omnipresence.

Be at peace.

The Spirit Calls

The Spirit calls out to me. For too long, I have blocked the voice. I have covered my ears. I covered my eyes. I have lived in the darkness. Moment by moment, I hear the voice becoming louder and louder. I cannot ignore it anymore. It is speaking from the depths of my being.

I am here. Listen. The words echo within. Listen, I am here.

I am here. I am with you. Listen. Feel me from within. Feel the deep longing to be in this Oneness of the Spirit within. Follow me in.

It calls me. It is so enticing. There can be no resistance. I long for it with every fibre of my being. Come, come to me. I take another step. Another step. Each one leads to another. I step deep into the unknown.

I cannot see the next step. I cannot see where it is leading me. I cannot see it for now. It is just mine to trust. To trust that the next step is there. I move each foot forward in total trust.

The pathway is becoming clearer. The fog is lifting in my mind. I live where I feel. I live in this truth, in this light. There is nothing else. As I move further within, deeper and deeper, this world disappears, and I step into the holiness of all. I step into the magnitude of infinity. I step into the Oneness of All.

There is nothing else. Nowhere else for me to be.

Flow of Grace

I allow God's grace to flow through me. I trust in its presence. I know that it fills my being. It supplies me with everything I need. It allows my life to go on and for me to be.

Can I be an instrument of this Grace? Can I be this presence? Can I allow it to flow through me, into others, throughout the earth? Can I give my all? Can I truly allow this to flow into all eternality?

Let it flow through me.

Guide me through this day. Allow the Grace to flow through me to everyone I see. Let me be tuned to the Spirit, so I may be an instrument of thy Grace.

Infinite Love

I Spirit am here in every moment. I live and breathe all. There is no separation, no difference, no opposite. I am all that there is. One. Walk in this Oneness at all times. Don't divide. Be still in this, for I am.

You cannot send me away. You cannot walk away. I will never leave you. Where ever you go, whatever you do, I am there with you in every step. There is nowhere to run to that I won't be there. I am a part of you. There is no division. Feel it. Know it.

I am the light that shines within you. The soul of you that shines out to the world. I will always be that. You try to cover it up and hide it, but there are always cracks, and I come through. People do see the Truth, the lies within you. They will see the infinite love that shines through. Do everything from this infinite love. When you let the love shine through, it will make the impact that is needed. Always be in this place of Infinite Love. This is who you are.

Be Still

Feel into the silence. Here is where the Truth lies. Your Truth that you cannot deny. Let your mind and thoughts dissipate into the silence. Silence is not being quiet but being still. A stillness that takes you out of the world into your true beingness. The Truth of who you are.

You are not this crazy, mixed-up person who is confused and forever running from place to place. You are not the fear that wells up inside of you. You are not the wants and desires of this world that you have to push and strive for.

Be still.

You are the One. Yes, you. When you stop and be still and feel into the silence, you will find yourself. You will find this Oneness that cannot be denied.

It is here that you will find peace.

It is here that you find love.

It is here that you find wholeness.

It is here that you find the Truth of who you are.

You are the wonderful child of the Universe that is One with all.

You and I are One. There is no separation. There is just this Oneness that expands throughout eternity. It always was and will always be. The small, the big, the good, the bad, the sick, the healthy, the fear, the unknown, it is all this One that is you.

Do not live in fear.

Live in love. Love for all, for all, is One. This One that is you.

Be still.

Fill Me

Fill me with your infinite Spirit. Be my life. Be my all. Take my life and make it an instrument of your love. Take all of it and fill it with your Will. I offer it freely, with confidence and assurance. I give my all to you with love.

Let my life be a testament to your Love and Grace. Let all that flows through me be yours. Hold me in your love so that all that I am is you. I give of my allness. I give to the Spirit my everything.

Let it shine through me. Let it be my everything. Let your Will be done through me.

In the silence.

Infinite Magnificence

It's a cold brisk morning in the Yarra Valley. The grass is covered in dew, the sun is shining, and birds are in full chorus. It is beautiful. I often resist running on these mornings as it is freezing. However, this morning it didn't even occur to me. I just went.

I stopped on the bush track to catch my breath. I looked up at the trees with the sun shining through and fell into the spell of Infinite Magnificence. How beautiful, how breathtaking was this moment of connection with all that is. I allowed this to flow through me. Who am I to stop this flow? This flow of all desires only to bless and provide for my every need. Who am I to stop this flow of what comes through me? The words I write, the words I speak. The provisions before me. The blessings of friends, family and community that have filled my life this week. The joy of connecting with friends in person after such a long break from physical contact.

Yes, who am I? I am not a being of limitation and lack that has to strive and push to survive and thrive. I am the flow of the Spirit, this Infinite Magnificence that takes me to places unseen, unthought of. I just need to allow this flow. To recognise the Spirit in all, that is all. To see it, feel it, know it.

It is not something I need to search for. It is not something I have to work for. It is. It is the essence of who I am, and who you are. It is. All I need to do is to let go. Let go of what I have created that blocks its flow through me. Let go of the world that demands so much and gives so little in return. Just be in the splendour of what is.

My heart is full, my mind at peace and the flow of the Infinite Magnificence is present. Always present.

Time to Be with God

I often sit and wait, and many times I forget to. It is time to sit and be with the presence. Time to be with God. Time to be in the Oneness. I can do nothing else but this.

It is what fills me. It is what takes my hand and guides me. I just have to reach out my hand, for it is always waiting for me. I reach out my hand. Please guide me today. I cannot walk alone. There is too much to do. The day is too long. There is only one way to do this. To do this with God.

I sit and wait. God, I don't know what to do. Take my will and transform it. Let my only will be to do your Will. Remind me again and again and again. Don't let me go. Don't let me waver. Don't let me turn away. Hold on to me, for I am yours and give to you freely. I am yours.

Come Sit with Me

Come sit with me. Just be here with me. Tell me about your day. Tell me how you feel, or just sit with me. I love to feel your presence. We don't need to talk if you don't want to. The love I have for you fills the silent moments.

Tell me of your worries and concerns. I will listen. Let go of the world, and then we can sit together and feel the peace. Surrender into the silence and the love I surround you with.

Tell me about your hopes and dreams. I will listen. Then let go. Sit in the quiet with me. Listen. Feel my presence. When you let go of what you want and listen, you may start to hear what I have for you. It is beyond your imagination. The blessings I have for you are more than you could have ever dreamed. But first, you need to let go and listen.

Come sit with me. In the stillness, we will find each other. In the quiet, you will get to know me. In the peacefulness, you will find that you and I are one. In the surrendering of all, you are blessed.

Come sit with me.

Live in Grace

It is a beautiful day. I feel the sun on my body, and the chill leaves it. The warmth sinks into the depth of my being. I surrender to its warmth and feel the blissfulness of being. In this moment, there is nothing else. Just surrendering. Just being. Feel the freedom of the surrender.

There is no need to fight. No need to strive or overcome. There is nothing but this moment in peace and in time. I feel its warmth, its blissfulness, its surrender. I am at peace.

God's love fills me just like this. I surrender into his arms, into his Grace, into his Oneness. I become one in his presence. I become one with all. I know, in this moment, that all is here. There is nothing else I can want, nothing else I can need. I have it all. I have it all in this moment.

God is. I surrender into the is-ness and know peace.

I live in his Grace.

The Word

The word fills me.

The word interrupts my being.

The word is all I need

The word is everything

The word is all

What more can I need besides the word?

It is me.

It is all.

It is everything.

Overflow

I watch the gentleness of the water flowing down the hill. It fills every crack in the ground, tumbling over stones and leaping over any obstacles. It doesn't stop. It just flows. The ground is quenched beyond its capacity. There is nowhere else for it to go, so the water flows.

The rain came and filled the watercourses. It overflowed the banks. The creeks and rivers filled and flowed on and on. This ever-present water flows on.

As I watch the water overflow, I think of the verse from Psalms "my cup overflows." I see how love can overflow. It fills you up, quenches your soul, and keeps flowing. It flows on and on. However, to start with, we have to open up to it. Open up that container and allow the water and love to enter. Then as it fills you up, it goes over the dam, allowing that water to flow beyond. Allow it to continue to flow. Without flow, it just grows stagnant and gets smelly and infested.

Allow it to flow. Trust that the rain will continue to fill up your dam and overflow into the world. The more we let it flow, the more we can accept and share.

Let it flow. Let the love that holds you, that uplifts you, that fills you, flow through you.

Freedom

What is freedom? My soul fills me with the thought, the feeling, the knowledge. My true freedom comes from the surrender, the totally surrender into my Spirit.

I do not need to worry, stress, to strive. Everything is here. Everything has been done. There is nothing that has not been taken care of. All I have to do is flow freely into the stream.

Let it all go. Let go of all the thinking, or all the planning, of all these "I must-dos" just be. Be in this presence. Be in this now. Be this. Let go of everything else and just be. Be free.

I Felt Like an Intruder

The morning sun was shining through the trees. The air was crisp and fresh. It was the perfect morning for a walk in the bush. I tried to pick out all the different birds' songs as they woke to the day. The sound of the magpies carolling dominated as their young fledging called out for food.

As I walked along the track, I started to feel like an intruder. It was not just the birds out for the morning. The kangaroos stood upright from their breakfast of fresh dew-covered grasses, disturbed by my presence. They stood still and looked at me. It becomes a stand-off. Am I going to keep going, or will I turn around? They stare at me intently. They want to stay. While I'm nowhere near them, it is clear that my continuation in that direction will disrupt them and make them feel unsafe.

In every direction I go this morning, there are kangaroos. I stop, then walk slowly and gently on the earth. This is their home too. They just want to have their breakfast. Who am I to stop them?

I ponder the disruption of the earth. How do we walk on it? Do we take care not to disturb that natural process? As I watch a cockatoo screeching and swooping at a fleeing fox, I am reminded of how we just take over. We introduce things. We do things our own way. The way that will make us happy.

What if we just take a step back? Take a moment to enjoy things as they naturally flow through life. Take notice of how nature intended them to be, instead of taking over, instead of manipulating so it is our way, instead of being in control, seeing how we can support the process.

Our lives are made up of so much rush and hurry to get things done, to make things happen. Sometimes we just have to stop. Stop and watch the kangaroos as they munch happily on the grasses. Stop and listen to the birds as they feed their young. Stop and feel our own sense of wonder. Awaken to that and be an intruder no more.

I Have Given All to You

I have given all to you. It is here for you. Fill your life with this knowledge. You cannot want. Just live in this fullness. Right now. It is all that there is. I fill your life with these. Infinite blessings. It is all you need. Be this now. Be this eternality. It is all.

We Are One

I look into your eyes, and what do I see?
I see beyond all that you appear to be from the outside.
I see beyond that which appears to be.
I see into the depth and truth of who you are.
You are not this outer shell.
You are not black or white.
You are not your experiences.
You are not mother, daughter, father or son.
You are the Infinite. The Spirit. I see your soul.

It speaks to me. Through your eyes, I see the beauty of all reflecting back at me. I see the magnificence of the universe. I see you, the you that you truly are.

Not the human, but the Spirit. The one with all.

My soul, your soul, they are one.

We walk together. Where ever we may be. We are One. We cannot be separated. We cannot be anything less than this Oneness. We cannot be any more, as this Oneness is all. We are One. We will always be One. We cannot be a part. One.

Following the Path

I was woken early in the morning by the cat howling. "Can't I just sleep in one morning?" I got up and tended to his needs and climbed back into bed. Something else was now calling to me. "Get up and go outside. Go for a walk." Seriously, it isn't light yet. I'll get up soon.

"Get up, go outside." The words kept coming.

"In a few minutes",

"Get up"

"Just a minute."

Then the cat started howling again.

"OK, I get the message."

It is winter, and I usually leave going out for a walk or a run until the warmest part of the day. But clearly, today was going to be different. I rugged up, and off I went.

I started walking and took a different pathway than my usual 2 or 3. I was just following where I was guided.

I often feel this with life. Just surrender to where I am guided. I don't need to know the full details of the destination just as long as I know the next step—one foot in front of the other.

The journey takes me onto what is a well-trodden bush track. I have been here before, but not often. I just enjoy the walk in the early morning light. Listening to the birds start their day. Taking in the sight of wattle trees just beginning to blossom. I feel at peace with my uncertain direction.

Just ahead, I see there are two pathways. Which one will I take? I allow myself to be guided and continue. Further on, there is a minor pathway. Will I explore? Off I go. It doesn't go far until I see where it is going. No, this pathway is not for me. That's OK. Exploring the possibilities is allowable. It's good to see and know that it is not where I am to go.

Back on the well-trodden path, I come to another, only just recognisable track calling me. I follow. I don't know where this path will go. Gradually the track disappears, and I am left standing in the middle of the bush. What now?

I realise that eyes are watching me. The almost camouflaged kangaroos look at me with a look of "what are you doing here?" I return an unspoken message that I won't disturb them. Where do I go? Do I turn around and go back?

Oh, I know this feeling. As I stand on the edge of life, stand on the edge of the known, I constantly ask myself do I step forward or fall back into the safety of the well-trodden path.

"No, continue on your journey." Trusting this inner voice, I step into the unknown and continue. Climbing over logs, being careful with each step so as not to get caught up in the long grasses.

I am reminded to trust that inner guidance if I want to see something new and create something new. I have to be willing to step out into the unknown, forge ahead and create my own pathway that others can follow.

As I surrender to the blissfulness of my morning adventure, the message of the morning is clear to me. I don't need to know the destination or the route it will take me. Trust the guidance that comes and just take one step at a time.

As I returned to my gate, the rain set in.

Darkness of the Night

In the darkness of the night, you call my name. I follow your voice to search within.

There is so much darkness. So much fear. But there is light, and there is love.

What is greater? How can you live in the darkness when you are light? How can you live in fear when you are love?

In every moment, there is love. It fills my being. It expands to every far reach of the world. I see it moving through and to every individual spark of divine light. This light that you are. This light that has been shrouded in the darkness.

While it is the middle of the night, it is time to get out of bed. To go outside and seek the light. Look up into the sky and see that glowing light calling you. For it is calling you out of the darkness. It is calling you into the light and the love.

Here, there is no other. There is no pain. There is no fear. There is only this Oneness that cannot be divided, this eternal connection of all. It doesn't matter whom you might think you are or who the next person is. It doesn't matter what you think is happening in the world or what the next person thinks. We are one. We are the same light.

There is only light.

Feel this. Go deep within, amid the darkness and find that pure light of your soul. It will feed and nourish you with only love.

You are the light. You are love.

Fill My Cup

Fill my cup again and again.

You fill my cup, and it runs over. Let it flow from me like a well of everlasting love. I am your servant, and all you give me is for all. I can keep nothing for myself, for it is yours to share.

You want to keep giving to me continuously. You want to share all of abundance. If I keep it to myself, there is no room for all you have for me. You give to me so that I can give to others.

Share in this love. Share in this allness. Share in the everything of all time.

Take Me

Take me, God, and show me your way. What is your will? What is it you will have to be and do today?

Be still. I will guide the path. I am opening the doors for you; all you need to do is follow. I am the way. You are mine. It is all there before you. Just walk in the light.

Hold Me in this Moment

Hold me in this moment. Help me to stay in your presence. Sometimes I am weak and forget that you are holding me. I forget that I am the presence. I forget that you and I are one.

Remind me in every moment, and remind me in everything that I do. Remind me in everyone I see and interact with. Remind me of the fullness in the wonder of the Truth. Don't let me fall. Hold me as One. Right here, right now. I need to feel your continuous presence in my life. I need to know that this is now. This is Oneness. Hold me now into eternity where I surrender to the Love and Grace. I am this. I am this now.

Newness of the Day

In the newness of the day, I search for you. The things of this world come rushing too fast to take over my mind, energy, and time. I sit in silence. I try to push them away. It is Spirit that I long for. That stillness, the presence. I call it in. I want it to take over. I want it to be all that I am.

In this moment, I give in to it. I give in to the silence. I let it take me to where it wants to go. Letting go of my thoughts. Letting go of my busyness. None of it matters. Let it go.

I watch as the thoughts flow over me. They try to grab hold, but I just let go, and like the river's flow, they can't hang on. They have pulled away while I sit firmly on the rock that is my foundation.

In this silence, I can be in the allness of time and space. I can fill the Truth of the presence that fills me. It takes me beyond my imagination. It takes me beyond this world. All that is flows through me, it comes to me, and I let it go. I feel the Oneness of all.

In this moment, I am all that I need to be.

Let Go of the World

In the Oneness, I feel at peace. I am not there alone. I may sit alone, but I carry everyone I know with me there. I carry everyone that ever was. We are all here in this moment: the sad, the lonely, the oppressed, the oppressor, the loved, the hated, in the Oneness.

I think I am going here to be alone, to be one with God. Then silently, as I sink deeper into God's arms, I feel us. Everyone just melting into this moment.

Here in this Oneness, there is peace. There is healing. There is the ultimate infinity. We are all connected in this very moment of One.

I cannot see the individual. I cannot see just I. All I can feel is this total envelope of completeness with each and every one. In this human form, we appear separate. We think, we act, and we respond as individuals. However, when in the Oneness, the Truth is evident. There is no separation. We are all of the Spirit. We are the Spirit. The very soul of me is the very soul of you. Forever intrinsically linked as One.

Today I sit with you, whoever you are, whatever you have done, whatever you think of yourself and hold you here, at this moment, with me, with the One. We are One. Together we find the true peace that fills our very being.

Let go of the world. It tries so hard to pull you in, to keep you in its current, full of twists and turns that have you smash into rocks, tumble through the murkiness, and often you don't know which way you are going or even which way is up. You continue the struggle trying to swim to safety. Then you find some calm waters to rest in, but don't rest too long. There is another wave coming. Once again, you are in the tumult of the rough waters. Over and over again, this cycle happens. It never stops—time after time.

Let go of the world. Rest in the arms of the Spirit. Here it is peaceful and always calm. Here it is safe. You will find comfort.

Let go of the world to find what your heart truly seeks, that which is the deepest part of itself. Here in the safe waters, you can let go, knowing that the natural flow will take you to where you need to be. The flow of the Spirit that guides and gently carries you into still waters.

Let go of the world and find your safe haven. Be at peace and allow yourself to find that inner stillness.

Sing in Wonder

Let my heart sing out in wonder of the love that surrounds us.

Let my heart be freed by the Spirit that flows through it.

Let my heart give thanks for all that is.

There is much to be grateful for, rejoice in and sing praise about. However, my soul can't separate one from the other. There can be nothing in-between.

There can't be that space of something that does not fill my heart. This Divine Love that fills my being is all-embracing. All that is lives in this moment of peacefulness and awe.

There isn't this space between Spirit and not Spirit. It fills me with wonder and opens me up in to this presence. This moment takes me beyond this world.

There isn't this space that is emptiness. There can never be emptiness when I walk with the Divine. There can never be aloneness. There can never be separation.

There isn't this space that defines one from another. It is all filled with Love and Spirit.

Feel into the presence. Fill into the Oneness. Let your Spirit sing in the glory of all.

In the Silence, I Hear My Name

In the silence, I hear my name. I am being called, called into something beyond this world. Something that propels me beyond what I can see. Beyond what I can understand. My understanding is not enough. It is beyond my comprehension. But it is calling me.

Listen.

Listen to where it is guiding you. Listen to where you are to go. Listen to what you are to be, to what you are. It is all in this moment. Just listen. It will take you beyond time, beyond space, beyond this world. This is where you live. This is where you are at One with all. This is where the Truth of all is revealed.

Listen. The silence knows your name.

Listen. It will take you beyond. You are ready. You are called. This is your timing. Listen.

I Am the Infinite

When I try to fit in the world, I get lost,
When I try to put who I am in a box, I get lost,
When I try to figure out who I am, I get lost,

For I am the Infinite.

I am not of this world,
I am not in a box,
I am not what you see,

For I am the Infinite.

I am beyond this world,
I am beyond all boundaries,
I am beyond all humanness,

For I am the Infinite.

Don't look for me in worldly things,
Don't look for me in time,
Don't look for me within this body,

I can't be found there,
I am beyond all time, all boundaries, all human thought.

I am the Infinite.

Journey of Life

Life is a journey through the known. You are born, you live, you die. What is this journey? What is it all about? Does it have a purpose? Does it have meaning? The eternal search for the meaning of life takes you around in circles. There is an endless search for a more significant reason for what happens, and the things you endure. The pain and suffering that you see. What is it for? Why does it keep going around and around?

You wonder why. Why this? Why that? All you see is pulling at you for this endless fight. What are you fighting? Why are you fighting? Is it real? Does it exist?

Where is the peace? Where is that sense of peace that we all crave? The constant search for peace in the world does not lead to peace. The peace you seek is here. You don't need to set out to change the world. Stop looking to the world for your answers. The answers lie within. The peace that you seek can only be found from within.

This burning desire to be someone, to do something, and to make a difference, does not lead to peace and fulfilment. Let go and find this peace within. Then you will have the answer. Then the world starts to unfold before you. Your peacefulness transcends to others. Who you are, and the difference you make begins here. It begins on this journey within. You will start to see what it is for you to do and be. It is here.

You don't need to go on an endless search. Get off the merry-go-round and find the peace within.

Turn Within

Turn within. Stay in this place.

Move forward from this place.

Stay clear. It is my Will to be with you. To show you the way. Be in this place of goodness that delights and surprises you every moment. Be here with me, and I will lead you home.

Do not be concerned, do not worry or fear. It is opening up to you in the midst of all. You will shine through in every moment. Hold still and shine.

I am the source of energy that you need. The only source. I am the bread of life. You are fed and nourished from within. Believe in me. Believe in the power that is within. It is all that there is. Be here.

Love

Love. Where does it go? When I love, where is it? What is it? How can I define what it means to love, to be loved?

The love of God fills me, and it is never-ending. When I think I grasp what it is and how it feels, I discover something more. It is always something more.

It cannot be captured, held and put into a box. I cannot tie it up with a bow and keep it for myself. The more I try to hold it, the more it makes me release it.

I feel it fill me up, but then it expands my capacity. It overflows into everything. Everything I am. Everything I do. Everyone I see. There is no limit to this love. There can be no limit to my love.

As I let this love flow through me, all I can be expands. I am loved by this capacity called Infinity. The more I love, the more love I have to share. It grows and grows with each inward breath of love. It expands beyond with each outward breath.

As the Infinite Spirit loves me, the love I feel for myself grows. I take it in and see myself anew. I am worthy of all this love. I am love.

The love I feel for others grows. As Infinite Love takes hold, I see no separation. This Love encompasses us all. I can't help but love you. We are One in the Infinite Love.

The love within expands. The Infinite Love fills and overflows through me to you.

Breath of God

The morning's hue surrounds me. The air I breathe is the breath of God. It fills my being with sustenance. It fills my body with the nourishment it needs. I am alive. I take this fullness of God into my being and know that there is none other. Everything that *is* is right here.

It takes me and moves me. I am transformed by the presence. It fills my being. It takes me and moulds me into shape. It takes me and makes me into what it will. My will is gone. Only the Will of God remains. I listen. I listen intently. Where will your presence guide me to be? Where will your presence take me? I am yours. Do with me as you will.

Seeking

What am I seeking? The journey beckons me on. I hear it calling my name. I look for it. I search for the Truth of it. But what am I seeking?

The journey seems endless. We are all seeking, seeking this, something that seems so elusive. It keeps us on this constant quest—this quenchless thirst for something more, something else.

The next experience, the next goal achieved, the next dollar earned.

Another box ticked, a moment of satisfaction and then that emptiness returns, and the search is back on.

The journey seems long and arduous. There is always another battle to be won, a mountain to be conquered. We fight on and on. Going where?

Now that we've gone so far. The longest journey begins, journeying beyond where we ever thought we would be. It is the most challenging journey. It is the journey of your life. The journey that finds the Truth. It is the one that you have been seeking.

In the silence, the way becomes clear. It is a little foggy to start with, and the battles will seem endless. But when you least expect it, the cloud will begin to lift, and you will start to see the way.

When you stay on this journey, you will start to see what you have truly been seeking. It is the journey back home. It is the journey back to you.

Beyond this World

Beyond this world is the world I wish to live in. When I let go of this world, I can feel it. It calls for me constantly. It has no limitations. It has all I need. It fills my life with constant wonder.

How can I let go and allow myself to walk only in the world of Spirit? This one that calls me. It beckons me forward. It entices me through every step. Yet this world is pulling. It tries to pull me back into the material, into the musts and the shoulds. It wants to engulf me in a world of pain and struggle. I cannot stay in this place. The world of the Spirit is the only world. The only truth that can take the wholeness of me.

There is only one world. It is the one I live for.

Take My Hand

Take my hand, my child. I will keep you safe. There is nothing you can fear while I am holding you. We will walk together through the darkest nights, cross the bottomless chasms, navigate through the roughest terrains, the most treacherous of oceans and climb the highest mountains. I will always be there, holding your hand, keeping you safe.

Sometimes when the obstacles seem insurmountable, I will pick you up and carry you over them. Other times you will want to race ahead, thinking, "I've got this." However, be patient, my child. The road ahead will reveal itself all in good time. In my time.

I will open the doors where you didn't even see a door. You will be welcomed where you thought it was impossible. I don't do impossible. I make all things possible. You just need to trust in me.

Take my hand like a child, and I will guide you safely to where you are meant to be. It won't always be an easy journey, but you are always safe. For you are my child, and I will provide for you always.

Just take my hand. Trust in me, and you will see that you are magnificent beyond the magnificent.

Beyond

Listen to the voice within. Where is it leading you? Stop and really listen. Let go of the mind. Let go of the world. Where is it taking you?

Beyond the mind, beyond your will, is something more significant for you to be and do. Let go of whom you thought you were. Let go of all the premises, all the expectations and obligations. You are none of that.

Who you are is beyond time, beyond space, beyond this world. There is more for you to be. Are you ready to explore? Then let go and delve into the silence. It is ready to guide you.

Something New to Be Born

Looking outside my window, I see the elm tree standing almost naked in the greyness of the morning. It is not like it was yesterday. Yesterday it was covered with far more leaves dancing in the sunlight. It surrendered its leaves. It surrendered them to the wind, to the change of season. It has let go of what it was yesterday.

Standing naked in the morning light, it takes in the moment of being still, allowing itself to be quiet. It is time to allow something new to be born within it. While all appears to be nothing, to be dead to the world, It is just resting.

It is in preparation for something new. It is preparing itself for new growth. It is strengthening itself in this rest. It will need so much energy and power from within to grow into a new season, a new season of abundance.

Abundance comes from within. I sit in stillness and contemplate.

Abundance and growth come from within. What can I need from the world when all is provided from within, from the Spirit that feeds my soul? Where I am today is perfect. As I surrender to letting go, my energies can be renewed. All that is new can start to flow. The growth starts from within. It may be hidden for a while. It may not show, but new growth is ensured when the sun begins to shine and winter turns to spring.

As I think about spring, I see the blossoms on the trees and the fruit that follows in abundance. It seemingly comes from nothing. All the tree has had to do is stand in the sunlight and allow the flow. It is deeply rooted in the earth. The ground gives it strength. It looks towards the sun to provide its direction. The air that it breathes provides it with life. All that is required to nourish its very essence surrounds it with abundance.

This thought comforts me. All that I need is within. I am filled with all my potential growth. I am fed and nourished. I have a direction to follow. All I need to do and be is here in this very moment. I can let go of yesterday, and all that was. All I need to do is surrender to the now. Just allow the flow.

It is time to rest with the Spirit that dwells within, for tomorrow's growth will require my all.

The Hidden Life

Sometimes, we are challenged to contemplate something in our life by watching a movie.

In watching "The Hidden Life", the true story of Franz Jägerstätter, an Austrian farmer, husband and father, during World War II, I had to ponder my own convictions. What do I stand for? Would my beliefs be unwavering, no matter what? Would I stand firm and not be shaken?

Franz was conscripted into the German Army. However, he refused to pledge allegiance to Hitler. He could feel and see underlying evil and would not be a part of it. He was thrown into prison, chained up constantly and frequently beaten. No matter what they did, he would not shift from his stand.

They offered him not to have to fight in combat but to be an orderly in a hospital. He asked, "Would I have to pledge allegiance to Hitler?" He remained in prison.

He was prompted," just sign this, and you will have your freedom."

"I am free," he responded.

Still locked up in chains, his heart and soul were free as he remained committed to his beliefs.

What is it that speaks to me so strongly? With an unwavering heart, do I stand steadfast in what I believe?

Will I hold fast to all that I stand for no matter what is presented to me by this world?

We often take what seems to be the easy way. It takes a lot of courage and strength to stand firm through moments of threat and difficulties. Then I question it. Through all the time Franz was imprisoned and continually threatened and beaten, would it have been any easier if he had given in to what was demanded of him? Wouldn't the other option of fighting a war, living in trenches, killing other people and quite likely being killed yourself be a more onerous burden to bear?

When you stand firm in what you believe, your heart is free. No matter what is thrown at you, something more substantial holds you up, holding you apart from the world. Even if your physical being is locked up in a prison cell and your hands are chained. There is something freeing about living up to what you believe.

Before he was executed, Franz wrote, "neither prison, nor chains, nor sentence of death, can rob a man of the Faith and his free will."

What do you stand for? What brings you freedom?

The Lighthouse

The lighthouse sits alone on the rocks. The wind blows, and the storm front beats against it, hurriedly forcing the waves onto the shore. It thrashes the building; it is not shaken. It stands steady. It stands steady against every storm. Whatever the weather throws at it, it bears the brunt—standing still in the midst of all. Whatever the sea throws at it, the most ferocious of waves, the hurricane-force wind, torrential hail and rain, it stands firm on its foundation.

The light shines on, regardless. It does not waiver in its commitment to shine a light to guide others safely on their journey. No matter what happens, that light must shine. It must guide them safely. It must be there to guide them home.

Being the light in the world does not exclude you from the storms. Quite often, it means that you are bearing the brunt of them. You are the one that holds still, so that others are protected and can find their way. You have built a strong foundation on the rocks, firmly grounded in your beliefs and structure. When others are falling by the wayside, you lift them. Shine your light and guide them to safety once again.

You have not been promised that it will be easy. If anything, you know that fixing yourself on the rocks means you will often be battered and bruised by the world. In the midst of the storm, you know that this is who you are. You know it is what you have chosen, and you know there is no place you'd rather be than being this light that guides others safely home.

You are the light. Continue to shine.

Silence

Silence. It beckons me through all time and space. I hear it whisper out to me, whispering my name. I listen. I listen harder. Can I hear it? Can I hear it speak to me through the noise of this world? Listen again. Stop the humdrum of the world. It knows nothing. It cannot feed or nourish you. The silence does.

Silence. Hear it. It calls to you from the deep, from beyond the horizon. Have you heard it? It knows your name. Your true name, your true identity. It knows your path, and your purpose. Silence. It will guide you if you will just listen.

Silence. It calls out to me. *"You are mine; I will hold you. Be not afraid, for we are one."* The silence and I are one. We move through all time together. There is nothing else—just silence.

Your Will

Where will your Will take me?

My heart is set on surrender. My greatest desire is to do your will. I let go and let go, and still, the world pulls me in. It tempts me away. Its busyness distracts me. It tells me that I must do things. That the things of the world need to be taken care of.

There are schedules and deadlines to make. People to take care of. Phones ring, and emails need to be answered. Life continues. It distracts me. It tries to make me forget, but you are here. Constantly that reminder sneaks in. There is something more, something greater, something more important than all of this.

Stop, surrender again. Feel the presence. Dissolve into it. Where is it that it is calling me to be? Where is it that it summons me to go? Who is it that I am called to be?

I surrender. I surrender unto you.

Spring is Budding

The morning is full of light, full of promise. As I gaze out my window at the new day, the budding of spring captures my sight. It captures my imagination for what is to come.

Winter, with its darkness and coldness, is fading. Those moments in time that seemed destitute with the blankness of the landscape. The fruit trees stood there naked, appearing dead to the world. It could have been so easy to abandon them, to feel that all was hopeless. There is nothing.

Slowly as the season began to turn, buds started to appear and blossom. Leaves are beginning to shoot again. Bees busily buzz around, collecting their nectar and ensuring we have the fruit that will sustain life. Soon we will have abundant fruit to share with the wildlife that gathers around.

As I ponder the season, I enjoy the delight of the new life. I see beyond the tree.

There are times we feel that we have lost hope. We think that we have nothing. Like the barren tree, there is no fruit. It appears nothing is happening. The tree asks for nothing. It stands there silently, knowing that all is right. This is a season, and the next will come without fail. It trusts that the water, the nutrients and the sunshine it needs will be provided. It trusts that the bees will be there to fertilise the blossoms.

In times that seemed so barren, did I trust something greater was going on? Something invisible was happening within, even though I could not see it with my physical eyes or hear it with my ears. It was something I needed to allow to flow and take its time, waiting for the sunshine for the light and the right season.

Then as if by magic, the buds begin to sprout, the blossoms bloom, the bees arrive, and the fruit emerges. Suddenly the abundance of life is evident. Life is sustained. All that I need is provided.

Who am I to doubt? The evidence stands in front of me in the beauty of the tree. Chaarlie.

Shallow Roots

The roots of the tree were shallow. It didn't take much for it to come down. The ground is saturated with water, and the wind continues to thrash at it. The trees that would naturally support it have all been removed. There is nothing left. It cannot survive on its own.

It was a warm still evening. We were sitting in our living room when we heard a sudden crack and thump. I knew what it was. Living this close to bushland, the sounds of trees falling has become all too familiar, especially this time of year. In springtime, we have heavy rain and powerful winds. It doesn't take much for the shallow-rooted gum trees to start falling.

Gum trees are notorious for falling. We know not to walk under them in a wind storm. However, it is often when all has gone quiet that suddenly they will come crashing down.

Their root structure isn't strong. For the height of the tree, you would expect the roots to go deep into the layers of the earth. The Messmate gum tree's support structure comes from having others around them. They need to feel the strength of the community holding them up. Together they stand firm. The wind can be savage to them, and drought hits, fires can rage through, yet strong, they stand together.

These two things cannot be underrated. I look around and see that many people don't have a strong root structure.

We need to go deep and form that solid foundation for support that sustains us. While our lives can appear to give us all that we need - food, water, ways to support ourselves financially - without this depth, we are vulnerable to the weather and the storms that come thrashing through.

When your roots are shallow, it is hard for you to stand up to all that comes at you. You have to battle the storm of life. You try to keep on going no matter what comes at you.

We have a choice, unlike the tree. We can choose to create deeper roots. We can choose to develop the support structure that each of us needs to survive the storms.

Deep roots mean that we can keep standing in the storms of life. We can shelter others around us safely.

We need to give attention to this system to give us the strength needed. We need to nourish and grow it, just like the tree that emerges from the soil. For some trees, this means pruning back and allowing the tree to withdraw from the seen world and focus on that deeper structure.

For those focused on growing into the depths, it often seems that not much is happening. However, deep within the ground, roots are growing stronger and stronger, deeper and deeper. They know that before they can spring forth above the ground, their roots need to be strong to weather the storms and grow to full capacity.

Grow your roots, work on your support structure, and you will weather the storms ahead.

Clear My Mind

Clear my mind of the world. It cannot hold me. It keeps trying to bring me back into the world. Clear this space. Let me walk in Spirit. I walk in the oneness of the day. I walk in the fullness of the light. Let me walk in the spirit.

The world tries hard to pull me back in. Each and every day, it fills my mind with something new. It fills it with fear. It fills it with love. It fills it with desire. It is all so tempting to fall back into the simplest of being. Believing what it shows me—falling back into the struggle and striving. But it is not me.

I walk in the Spirit. I let go of the day and walk in the presence. I give my life to this Oneness of all.

The world has disappeared.

Only Love

There is love. Only love. It is all we need to focus on. It is all we need to be. Everything else flows when we have true love, which expands through us to all reaches of our being.

There is love, and then there is LOVE. Human love can be selfish and so easily abused. It can fill us with jealousy and resentment. It has an opposite, that of hate. Then it becomes a dangerous tool.

Whereas LOVE is pure. It is whole and all-inclusive. There is no room for an opposite. LOVE fills every gap and every part of your being. It flows into all corners of the universe. In it, you feel whole. You are complete. In LOVE, there is only ONE. The Oneness that you feel that transcends our daily lives. It fills our being. It takes over our lives.

That really is the key, isn't it? To allow it to take over our lives. Surrendering into the LOVE and allowing us to be the one and only focus of our very soul. This is what you are here for. You are here to reconnect with this LOVE. To feel it, allow it to flow to you and through you, to give it with all of your might. When you give this LOVE, you can't help but receive it back, for this is all there is. You can never run out of LOVE. It keeps refueling itself.

Let yourself be LOVE. Breathe it in with every breath. Breathe it out unto the world. This is who you really are. LOVE

This Is the Moment

This is the only moment. It appears at a moment in time, yet it is the only moment. It is the moment to be. The moment to put aside all things and just be. Listen to the moment. It is speaking to you. It is speaking beyond time. For at this moment, all time exists. All things are known.

You were born for this moment. Right here, right now.

Where are you? Is there anywhere else to be but right here in this moment? The past has never been. The future will never be. There is only right now.

Call out to your soul in this moment. What do you want of me? Who am I in this moment?

In this moment, you are all that you can be. Infinite. Magnificent. Unlimited. In this moment, all that is is available to you. It is yours. Reach out for it is calling you into the fullness of being.

Don't deny this gift. It is yours. It wants nothing but to love you. It wants only for you to be in the allness of your being.

Take this moment and live it. Take this moment and know it is yours. Take this moment and know that right here, right now, you are infinitely magnificent.

All that *is* is yours in this moment.

You Are Called

You are called by something greater than yourself. The infiniteness calls you from beyond this moment in time. There is something greater, something magnificent that you have not yet seen. It is calling you from beyond the why.

We live in this world that has us struggling and striving. Our bubble of thinking keeps us within this place of being enough. It constantly tells us that we must be more, do more, and have more. Yes, you tell yourself, "I am enough."

But there is something more significant. It is time to burst the bubble. The only belief that limits you is the belief that you are limited. What lies beyond is infinitely magnificent. Open up into this power that is yours to behold. However, you cannot work for it. You cannot plan for it. You cannot strive for it.

For it is you. It is you now, and it will always be you. Let it be you. When you let go of all that is of the world, surrender to the silence, to the Oneness, you can feel this aliveness that needs and wants for nothing. In this beingness, you feel the Infinite, the Allness, the Isness. Here is where you start to see the magnificence of who you are.

Surrender into it. Relax into your Spirit and find the Infinite Magnificence that is you.

What Is Love?

Love. What is love?

My love for you expands. It encompasses all.

My love is strong and overpowers me. I can't do anything else but love.

My love grows and grows, minute by minute, second by second. It lives within me. It lives through every fibre of my being. It is who I am.

My love is expansive. There is no limit. I give it to you freely. It comes with no obligation, no requirements. You don't have to love me back. You don't have to do anything for me. It is yours. IThet is your gift.

I give it to you. I give my all. All that I am is here. All that I am is freely given. It is who I am, the truth. The one. The whole.

I am this love. It fills me. It frees me. It frees you. It doesn't hold you in some cage. It sets you free in the wind. Go and fly, for I believe in you.

It is you I love, be love, be free.

Warm Cup

As I sit with my warm cup in my hands, the world fades away. I find myself inside of me. Not the me of the world, but the I of the soul. There are no words. There is no thinking. There is just the peace of the moment that fills me.

I take this moment and surrender in to it. Where will it take me today? Where will it lead me? I can have no agenda. I can have no plans. Just take me away to this place where I feel filled with peace.

In this moment, there can only be Oneness. The me dissolves into all.

There is nothing I need. There is nothing I want. There is nothing I have to do. It is all just here. All. Everything I need to know is right here in this moment. Everything I need to be is right here in this moment. I am in the allness of my being.

Just me and my warm cup of tea, surrendering into a moment of infinity.

Index

A Moment Ago, 91
Allness, 88
Autumn Leaves, 22
Be In the Presence, 64
Be Present, 79
Be Still, 9, 96
Beyond, 127
Beyond the Horizon, 48
Beyond this World, 125
Breath of God, 123
Carry Me Today, 70
Clear My Mind, 139
Come With Me, 49
Darkness, 53
Darkness of the Night, 111
Day After Day, 63
Do Not Rush Today, 81
Doors, 26
Fill Me, 97
Fill My Cup, 112
Fill My Heart with Awe, 61
Find Me, 41
Flow of Grace, 94
Following the Path, 108
Freedom, 104
God's Day, 20
Good Morning God, 60
Grace Accepts Me, 28

Guide me, 21
Hold Me in this Moment, 113
Home, 43
I Am I, 71
I Am One, 31
I Am the Infinite, 119
I Am Yours, 73
I Can't Not Do It, 35
I Dwell In the House of the Lord, 56
I Felt Like an Intruder, 105
I Have Given All To You, 106
I Hear You Call Me, 12
I Seek My Path, 57
I Sit With You God, 59
I Spirit Am Here, 90
I Will Guide You, 60
In the Silence I Hear My Name, 118
Infinite Love, 95
Infinite Magnificence, 98
Journey of Life, 120
Juice, 46
Just a Minute, 50
Just breathe, 69
Lead Me By Still Waters, 23

Lean In, 66
Let Go of the World, 115
Let It Flow Through Me, 75
Let Your Light Shine, 16
Let Your Love Shine, 15
Light Creeps Through, 38
Light Finds a Way, 78
Listen Beyond Hearing, 34
Live in Grace, 101
Love, 122
Love Divine, 72
Magnificent, 27
Middle of the Night, 17
Moment of Infinity, 11
My Child, 14
My Heart Calls For You, 87
Newness of the Day, 114
No Words, 13
Now In This Moment, 82
One, 14
Oneness, 68
Only God, 74
Only Love, 140
Overflow, 103
Peace, 19
Perfectly, 13
Ponder, 62
Pull Up the Anchor, 42
Reflections, 30
Relax In the Spirit, 64
Rest In My Arms, 33
Rest in the Spirit, 36
River Flow, 37

Seeking, 124
Shallow Roots, 137
Silence, 133
Sing in Wonder, 117
Sitting in the Light, 86
Something New to Be Born, 128
Soul Dweller, 77
Spirit Fill me, 58
Spirit Flow Through Me, 76
Spring is Budding, 135
Start with God, 29
Stay in Tune, 85
Stepping Forward, 25
Surrender, 92
Take Me, 113
Take My Day, 84
Take My Hand, 126
The Edge, 47
The Hidden Life, 130
The Lighthouse, 132
The Moment Has Come, 55
The Mountain Top Calls Me, 67
The Narrow Path, 83
The Rain, 54
The Spirit Calls, 93
The Word, 102
This Is the Moment, 141
Through the Fog, 32
Time to Be with God, 99
Timeless, 65
Trust the Process, 39
Turn Within, 121

Waiting, 24
Walk In the Light, 15
Warm Cup, 144
We Are One, 107
What Do You Want?, 80

What Is Love?, 143
With You Always, 44
Wonder, 45
You Are Called, 142
Your Will, 134

ABOUT THE AUTHOR

Andrea Putting is an international speaker, author and trusted advisor to those seeking to make a difference in the world. Her lifelong journey of Spirituality has guided her to a deep listening of the soul.

Her writings have inspired and challenged people online and in print for over 20 years. Andrea's blog, *Putting Perspective*, covers an arena of topics from Spirituality to community and business.

Andrea's books, *Awakened Stealth Leadership – A Soulful Approach to Growing People and Organisations* and *Compassionate Prosperity - When Success is Not Enough*, focus on living a more conscious life in business. Her book *Compassionate Purpose – Discovering a Life of Fulfilment* takes readers on a journey to discover their personal and fulfilling mission in life. She is a best-selling and award-winning author and wordsmith who has co-authored collaborative books.

Andrea is the founder of Chocolate and Coffee Day for Religious harmony and Chocolate and Coffee Breaks. These events encourage people to share chocolate, coffee and conversation with the intent of breaking down barriers that divide people and community.

Since 2019, Andrea has been championing the causes of passionate people making a difference in the world through her podcast, *Social Mission Revolution.* The podcast highlights inspirational people and businesses who have an Authentic influence on the world through social mission.

Andrea Putting lives in Melbourne, Australia, amongst the gumtrees, kangaroos and cockatoos with her husband and pet cockatoo, Fella. She has two adult children and two grandchildren who keep her jumping in puddles.